Th
Trials
of
Oscar
Wilde

Merlin Holland
& John O'Connor

SAMUELFRENCH-LONDON.CO.UK
SAMUELFRENCH.COM

FOR AMATEUR PRODUCTION ENQUIRIES

UNITED KINGDOM AND WORLD EXCLUDING NORTH AMERICA
plays@SamuelFrench-London.co.uk
020 7255 4302/01
UNITED STATES AND CANADA
info@SamuelFrench.com
1-866-598-8449
Each title is subject to availability from Samuel French, depending upon country of performance.

Author's note by Merlin Holland

One of the most famous love affairs in literary history is that of my grandfather, Oscar Wilde, and Lord Alfred 'Bosie' Douglas. They had met in 1891, not long after Wilde had published *The Picture of Dorian Gray* to a storm of critical abuse, and for nearly four years they conducted a tempestuous love affair. Bosie's father, the Marquess of Queensberry, had tried to force his son to put an end to what he saw as their 'disgusting relationship', but unable to do so, he decided to bring matters to a head by leaving a badly spelled visiting card at Wilde's club on 18 February 1895, a few days after the opening night of *The Importance of Being Earnest,* accusing him of being a 'somdomite'. Wilde, egged on by Douglas, who detested his father and wanted nothing better than to see him behind bars, took the bait, the 'booby trap' as Queensberry later called it, and decided to sue the Marquess for criminal libel. It promised to be one of the most sensational trials of the decade – an upstart Irish playwright taking an irascible Scottish aristocrat to court – but it set in motion a train of events which were to cost Wilde his freedom, his reputation, his art and ultimately his life.

The case opened on 3 April, with Wilde confidently expecting to win by wittily justifying his literature and his lifestyle. However, he had not reckoned with the damning evidence of the young men, the rent-boys and the blackmailers, which the defence lawyers had unearthed in London's homosexual underworld. He had also underestimated the forensic ability of Queensberry's counsel, Edward Carson. Under powerful cross-examination the roles of prosecutor and accused were effectively reversed, with Wilde in the witness box becoming the defendant in his own action. As Wilde and Carson duelled for the playwright's reputation, the exchanges between the two Irishmen became increasingly heated. Wilde's confidence ebbed under Carson's relentless cross-questioning. Those witty lines and epigrams which had made him so famous, were now disastrously out of place in the courtroom, and Wilde effectively talked himself into prison.

On the third day of the trial, Wilde withdrew his prosecution after the defence, in justification of the libel, had started to reveal the extent of their witnesses' testimony. But as an exercise in damage limitation it was a failure, for Queensberry then instructed his solicitors to send all their evidence to the Director of Public Prosecutions and Wilde was arrested the same evening. Within three weeks he was back in the Old Bailey, this time in the dock, charged with 'gross indecency with other male persons' under Section 11 of the 1885 Criminal Law Amendment Act. The jury failed to agree on a verdict; a retrial was ordered and on 25 May (less than 100 days after the opening of *Earnest*) he was sentenced to two years imprisonment with hard labour.

But what actually took place in the court-room and behind the scenes during those seven weeks? The Old Bailey Sessions Papers, which normally gave detailed summaries of most cases simply said of the libel trial 'The details of the case are unfit for publication' and of the two subsequent prosecutions by the Crown they gave the barest of details in a few lines. The newspapers were less squeamish, but their reports were necessarily shortened versions of the proceedings and filled with circumlocutions like 'unnatural practices' and 'indecent acts'. It wasn't until 1912 that *Oscar Wilde Three Times Tried* was published anonymously, purporting to give an accurate record of the trials in order to dispel the 'vague fog of obscenity' surrounding them. No sources were given for the material but most of it seems, on analysis, to have been gleaned from contemporary newspapers, though still 'with due regard to discretion'. That record was reprinted more or less word for word in 1948 in the Notable British Trials Series and, in the absence of any other documents preserved at the Old Bailey or in the National Archives, it remained the only account of Oscar Wilde's trials for the next fifty years.

It was in 2000, while I was helping prepare an exhibition at the British Library to commemorate the centenary of my grandfather's death, that someone appeared in the Library with the shorthand transcripts of the libel trial as a possible exhibit. There are moments of discovery in any research field which are akin to the euphoria of sporting triumph or sexual climax; this was one. If there was a Holy Grail of Wilde studies, finding his words taken down in shorthand at one of the major events in his life would come quite high on the list of nominations. The elation once over I started to assess the implications. For a start we now had nearly 85,000 words as against the mere 30,000 known until then and having Oscar's own words rather than paraphrases or, even worse, words he never uttered, put him in a rather different light. Far from starting his examination-in-chief with a boastful catalogue of his achievements: 'I am the prosecutor in this case . . . I took a classical scholarship and the Gold Medal for Greek,' and so on, he simply answers the relevant questions put by his counsel with a sober 'Yes' or 'I did'. This was a gift when John O'Connor and I came to dramatizing the proceedings as it provided a natural crescendo from demure and then confident, through recklessly witty (Did you ever kiss him – Oh, no, never in my life: he was a peculiarly plain boy), to flustered and unnerved. He also spends more time than we previously thought defending his writings against the charges of immorality and obscenity as well as declaring under cross-examination that he loved Alfred Douglas, a statement totally absent from all printed accounts until then. It is those transcripts which form the basis of Act I of this play.

Apart from being able to use the very words which Wilde uttered in court, the other major difference between this and previous attempts to present Wilde's trials as drama for the stage, lies in the way they were abridged. In the course of the three cases, Wilde spent more than eight days in the Old Bailey and to reduce this to a mere two hours of well-paced theatre required the art of the surgeon's scalpel rather than the butcher's cleaver. Essentially there were three main elements to each trial: Wilde's relationship to Douglas; his defence of his art; and his consorting with rent-boys and blackmailers. Each had to be represented in the right proportion and with extracts long enough to keep as much of the natural dramatic tension as possible, then the components sewn back together to form a credible whole. The result, as Peter Ackroyd said of the published transcripts, is as good as being in the gallery.

If I could ask my grandfather a single question, it would have to be: 'Why on earth did you do it?' Even if there is no simple answer, there is a blindingly obvious explanation. Looking back over a century, and especially the last thirty years in British Courts, it comes as no surprise to see how little has changed whenever fame, sex, pride and libel are shaken up into their intoxicating cocktail of human weakness. The outcome is as predictably fascinating for the onlookers, as it is invariably disastrous for the participants.

So when the Irish Peacock took the Scarlet Marquess to court, he took on the British Establishment and passed, as he said, 'from an eternity of fame to an eternity of infamy'. It was his last public appearance as a free man, but his fight, although insanely quixotic, was fought with all that style and conviction which we have come to expect from Oscar Wilde.

Merlin Holland, September 2014

Author's note by John O'Connor

Is there anything we don't know about Oscar Wilde? He is quoted endlessly and his plays are always in fashion. There are countless biographies, documentaries, films and songs about the great man. Social media are full of Wildean quotes which fit neatly into 140 characters and his image is as famous as Che Guevara or James Dean.

For all those reasons, staging this play can present an exciting challenge. Audiences think they know Oscar personally but what this story reveals is how richly complex and maddeningly contrary he was. We tend to think of Wilde speaking entirely in elegantly constructed epigrams but here are his actual words spoken off-the-cuff and under pressure. He evades, lies, deflects and eventually stumbles into incoherence, but also displays those flashes of lightning for which he is rightly famous.

The part of Oscar is a great test for an actor. It needs someone who can convey his wit, warmth, mercurial mind, mastery of language, grandiosity, dignity and paradoxical nature. During the play, Wilde goes from brashly confident to bravely defiant to a man broken on the wheel of Victorian hypocrisy. Was there ever a more rapid, dizzying fall from grace outside one of Shakespeare's tragedies?

Aside from in a West End theatre, the play has been performed in a converted church, a wooden barn, a Victorian courtroom, a high school and even a Scottish cattle byre. It can work almost anywhere on most stages, with a cast as small as three or as large as eighteen as your budget allows. A smaller cast will convey the claustrophobia of the courtroom while a larger one will highlight the whole colourful circus that surrounded the trials.

We chose to use the audience as the jury which involves them in the action and makes them part of the drama. But which ever way you choose to approach the play, what ultimately compels an audience for two hours is that this story takes in big themes – freedom of expression, the class system, the artist versus the state, morality and immorality, and the right of one human being to love another.

Things have moved on a long way since Oscar was on trial. However, it's important to remember that elsewhere in the world artists and writers are regularly imprisoned for being thorns in the side of the establishment. And according to the charity Stonewall, it is still illegal in 78 countries to be gay and in five of those it is punishable by death. In that context, this is a story that urgently needs to be told.

John O'Connor, September 2014

THE TRIALS OF OSCAR WILDE

The play was first presented by European Arts Company at the Hazlitt Theatre, Maidstone on 3rd May 2014 before touring to 43 venues all over the UK. It subsequently transferred to Trafalgar Studios in London and opened on 13th October 2014 with the following cast of characters:

Oscar Wilde . . . . John Gorick

The Marquess of Queensberry . . . . Rupert Mason
Edward Carson
Alfred Wood
Charles Gill
Jane Cotter
Fred Atkins
Auctioneer
Judge
Foreman of the Jury

Sir Edward Clarke . . . . William Kempsell
Charles Parker
William Allen
Arthur
Antonio Migge
Sidney Wright
Policeman
American Reporter

Producer – John O'Connor
Director – Peter Craze
Designer – Dora Schweitzer
Lighting Designer – Duncan Hands
Sound Designer – Derek Carlyle

The Trials of Oscar Wilde

by Merlin Holland
and John O'Connor

CHARACTERS

In order of appearance

OSCAR WILDE

POLICEMAN

MARQUESS OF QUEENSBERRY

SIDNEY WRIGHT

SIR EDWARD CLARKE QC

EDWARD CARSON QC

ALFRED WOOD

WILLIAM ALLEN

ARTHUR (WILDE'S MANSERVANT)

AMERICAN REPORTER

AUCTIONEER

CHARLES GILL QC

CHARLES PARKER

JANE COTTER

ANTONIO MIGGE

FRED ATKINS

JUDGE

FOREMAN OF THE JURY

The play can be performed with a minimum of three actors, a full complement of eighteen or anything in between. The action takes place in London between 14 February and 25 May 1895. The script is based on the words spoken in court during the libel trial and two subsequent criminal trials at the Old Bailey in 1895. A full transcript of the libel trial was published by Merlin Holland in *Irish Peacock and Scarlet Marquess: the Real Trial of Oscar Wilde* (2003). The transcripts of the criminal trials have never been found so we have used Christopher Millard's *Oscar Wilde Three Times Tried* (1912), as well as eyewitness accounts and contemporary newspaper reports to piece together what was said in court. We have also used some of Wilde's own words from his letters and *De Profundis*. There are several quotations from *The Importance of Being Earnest*, which opened on 14 February 1895 at the St James's Theatre and closed after just eighty-two performances because of the trials. Wilde's curtain speech is actually taken from the opening night of *Lady Windermere's Fan* (1892) as he didn't make a speech after the triumphant opening night of *Earnest*.

We have merged the two criminal trials into one as the evidence heard in both was similar. In the first (26 April - 1 May 1895) the prosecution was led by Charles Gill and the jury could not agree a verdict. A retrial was ordered (22 - 25 May) and this time the prosecution was led by the Solicitor General himself, Sir Frank Lockwood. For reasons of clarity, we have named the prosecutor solely as Charles Gill but the evidence and cross-examination is taken from both trials.

ACT I

Scene 1 – Interior of St James's Theatre.
14 February 1895

Blackout. We see **OSCAR WILDE** *waiting in the wings and hear the sound of laughter. Then a voiceover of the last lines from* The Importance of Being Earnest.

GWENDOLEN. Ernest! My own Ernest! I felt from the first that you could have no other name!

JACK. Gwendolen, it is a terrible thing for a man to find out suddenly that all his life he has been speaking nothing but the truth. Can you forgive me?

GWENDOLEN. I can. For I feel that you are sure to change.

JACK. My own one!

LADY BRACKNELL. My nephew, you seem to be displaying signs of triviality.

JACK. On the contrary, Aunt Augusta, I've now realised for the first time in my life the vital Importance of Being Earnest.

Laughter. Wild applause. Calls of 'Author'. **WILDE** *walks on stage to take the curtain call.*

Lights up on the other side of the stage to reveal the **MARQUESS OF QUEENSBERRY** *standing outside the theatre. We can still hear the sound of applause.*

POLICEMAN. I'm sorry Lord Queensberry, I have strict instructions not to allow you in.

QUEENSBERRY. Then make sure that Wilde receives these as a token of my esteem!

He hands the **POLICEMAN** *a bouquet of rotten vegetables. Lights fade out.*

WILDE *on stage as the applause fades.*

WILDE. Ladies and gentlemen: I have enjoyed this evening *immensely*. The actors have given us a *charming* rendering of a *delightful* play, and your appreciation has been *most* intelligent. I congratulate you on the great success of your performance, which persuades me that you think almost as highly of the play as I do myself.

He bows. The applause is even louder this time and mingled with cheers. He drinks in the adulation and the lights fade.

Scene 2 – The Albermarle Club. Morning

SIDNEY WRIGHT *the hall porter is behind a desk, enter* **QUEENSBURY**.

WRIGHT. Excuse me Sir, this is members only… oh, I'm sorry my Lord, I didn't recognise you.

QUEENSBERRY. I wish to see Mr Oscar Wilde. I believe he's a member of this establishment.

WRIGHT. I'm afraid he's not here at the moment, Lord Queensberry, and hasn't been in for a few days.

QUEENSBERRY. Bah!

WRIGHT. Can I take a message for you?

QUEENSBERRY. A message? Yes…yes… *(takes a pen and writes on the card)*… see that he gets this!

WRIGHT. Certainly Sir.

QUEENSBERRY exits. **WRIGHT** *glances at card and looks perplexed. He carefully places it in an envelope, seals it and writes on it.*

Music.

Scene 3 – The Albemarle Club. Afternoon

WILDE *enters the club.*

WRIGHT. Oh, Mr Wilde. Lord Queensberry left this for you.

WILDE *opens envelope and reads card. Music. The colour seems to drain from his face. He exits. Blackout.*

The indictment is heard in voiceover.

John Sholto Douglas, Marquess of Queensberry, you are charged with contriving and maliciously intending to injure Oscar Fingal O'fflaherty Wills Wilde*, and to deprive him of his good name, fame, credit, and reputation and to provoke him to commit a breach of the peace and to bring him into public contempt and disgrace on the eighteenth day of February in the year of our Lord one thousand eight hundred and ninety-five by unlawfully, wickedly and maliciously writing and publishing a false, scandalous and defamatory libel in the form of a card 'For Oscar Wilde posing as somdomite' meaning thereby that the said Oscar Wilde had committed and was in the habit of committing the abominable crime of buggery with mankind to the great damage, scandal and disgrace of the said Oscar Wilde, and against the peace of our Lady the Queen, her Crown, and dignity.

Scene 4 – The Old Bailey

CLARKE. I trust you are on good form and feeling confident Mr Wilde.

WILDE. Thank you, Sir Edward, yes. Of course the man's a complete lunatic. Inbred Scottish aristocrat.

---

* This was Oscar Wilde's full name until early 1877, after which he signed his name and referred to himself only as Oscar Wilde

CLARKE. That's as may be, but I'm somewhat concerned about last week's disclosures over young men...

WILDE. Oh, nothing but Piccadilly prostitutes – they sell their souls for pieces of silver.

CLARKE. But Edward Carson wouldn't have accepted the brief had he thought...

WILDE. Ned Carson and I go back a long way. We last crossed swords debating at university. He was always far too serious to be an effective orator.

CLARKE. That doesn't prevent him being a formidable lawyer.

WILDE. Yes, I expect he will perform his task with all the added bitterness of an old friend.

> **SIR EDWARD CLARKE** *opens the case for the prosecution.*

CLARKE. My Lord, I am for the prosecution and my learned friend, Mr Edward Carson, is for the defence. May it please your lordship, gentleman of the jury, you have heard that the charge against the defendant is that he published a malicious libel with regard to Mr Oscar Wilde. That libel was published in the form of a card, which was left by Lord Queensberry at the club to which Mr Oscar Wilde belongs.

Now, gentlemen, of course it is a matter of serious moment that such a word as Lord Queensberry had written on that card should in any way be connected with the name of a gentleman who has borne a high reputation in this country. It is not an accusation of the gravest of all offences – 'posing as a sodomite' indeed appears to suggest there is no guilt of the actual offence – but the publication of such a statement, the leaving of such a card with the porter of a club, is an act most serious, likely gravely to affect the reputation and the position of my client.

Mr Oscar Wilde is a gentleman of thirty-eight years of age at this time. You may possibly know that many years ago he became a very public person indeed, laughed at by some, appreciated by many but at all events representing a special and particular aspect of artistic literature, which commended itself greatly to many of the most cultivated people of our time.

In 1891, Mr Wilde made the acquaintance of a gentleman whose name I mention – it is necessary I should mention – Lord Alfred Douglas, the son of the defendant. Lord Alfred came to Mr Wilde's house in Tite Street one afternoon, introduced by a friend of theirs and from that time until now Mr Oscar Wilde has been friendly not only with Lord Alfred but also with Lord Alfred's brothers and his mother Lady Queensberry. Until the early part of the year 1893 Mr Oscar Wilde did not know the defendant at all with the exception that they seem to have met once a good many years ago, and of Lord Queensberry Mr Wilde saw very little until the early part of the year 1894.

He did become aware that some statements were made affecting his character – I do not mean by Lord Queensberry – but he became aware of it in this way. There was a man named Wood who had been given some clothes by Lord Alfred Douglas and who said that he had found in the pocket of a coat that was given to him four letters that had been written by Mr Wilde to Lord Alfred Douglas. Wood came to Mr Oscar Wilde early in the year 1893 and wanted Mr Wilde to give him something for the letters, saying he was in great distress and trouble and wanted to go to America. Mr Wilde gave him fifteen pounds to pay his passage and Wood handed to him three somewhat ordinary letters. A while later, one of Wood's accomplices called on Mr Wilde with the fourth letter and also wanted Mr Wilde to give him something for it. He absolutely and peremptorily refused, refused in terms which you will hear.

That original letter is in my hands now. He said then and he says now that he looks upon this letter as being a sort of prose-sonnet and that it would appear in sonnet form. It did so appear. I hold in my hand a copy of a publication, which was issued on the 4th May 1893 called '*The Spirit Lamp*. An aesthetic and literary magazine edited by Lord Alfred Douglas' and on the first page of it there is a sonnet which is thus headed:

WILDE. 'A letter written in prose-poetry by Mr Oscar Wilde to a friend and translated into rhymed poetry by a poet of no importance'.

CLARKE. It is in French. It is signed Pierre Louÿs and here is the letter. 'My own boy...

> **WILDE** *and* **CLARKE** *(together)*: 'Your sonnet is quite lovely...

> **CLARKE** *freezes and lighting is on* **WILDE** *through the reading of this.*

WILDE. ... and it is marvel that those red, rose-leaf lips of yours should be made no less for music of song than for madness of kissing. Your slim gilt soul walks between passion and poetry. I know Hyacinthus whom Apollo loved so madly was you in Greek days. Why are you alone in London and when do you go to Salisbury?

CLARKE. Salisbury was where Lord Alfred Douglas's mother lived.

WILDE. Do go there and cool your hands in the grey twilight of Gothic things and come here whenever you like. It is a lovely place: it only lacks you; but go to Salisbury first.

WILDE AND CLARKE. Always with undying love...

CLARKE. ... yours Oscar.' Now, gentlemen, the words of that letter appear extravagant to those who are in the habit of writing commercial correspondence or those ordinary letters, which the necessities of life force upon one every day, but that, Mr Oscar Wilde said then and says now – that is a sort of prose-sonnet and answer to a piece of poetry written by Lord Alfred Douglas. He preserved this letter until today and produces it now saying to you it is a letter of which he was, and is, in *no* way ashamed; that that letter has no relation whatever to the hateful suggestions – hateful to him as to all of you – which are made with regard to him in the plea in this case.

Gentlemen, we intend to prove the publication of the libel in question and my learned friend will have the task upon him, if he really proposes to address himself to that, of endeavouring to satisfy you by evidence that the accusations that they have made are true.

OSCAR WILDE *sworn*.

CLARKE. You are the prosecutor in this case?

WILDE. Yes.

CLARKE. I think you are thirty-eight years of age?

WILDE. I am thirty-nine years of age.

CLARKE. Was your father the late Sir William Wilde a surgeon in Dublin?

WILDE. He was.

CLARKE. Were you a student at Trinity College, Dublin?

WILDE. Yes.

CLARKE. And at that University or College did you obtain a classical scholarship and the Gold Medal for Greek?

WILDE. I did.

CLARKE. Then, I believe, you went to Magdalen College, Oxford and took a first in Mods and a first in Greats?

WILDE. Yes.

CLARKE. And obtained the Newdigate Prize for English Verse?

WILDE. Yes.

CLARKE. I believe as early as 1881 you published a volume of poems?

WILDE. I did.

CLARKE. Did you afterwards make a lecture tour in America?

WILDE. Yes.

CLARKE. And have lectured also in England, I think?

WILDE. Indeed.

CLARKE. During the last few years you have devoted yourself specially to dramatic literature?

WILDE. I have.

CLARKE. I think I am right in mentioning *Lady Windermere's Fan, A Woman of No Importance, The Importance of Being Earnest* and *An Ideal Husband* as the four plays of yours which have been interpreted on the stage in this country?

WILDE. Yes.

CLARKE. And all of them successful?

WILDE. They have all, I am glad to say, been successful.

CLARKE. In the year 1884 you married Miss Lloyd?

WILDE. Yes.

CLARKE. And from the date of that marriage up to now you have been residing with her at Tite Street, Chelsea?

WILDE. I have.

CLARKE. You have two sons?

WILDE. I have two sons.

CLARKE. Of what age?

WILDE. The eldest will be ten in June and the youngest will be nine in November.

CLARKE. In the year 1891 did you make the acquaintance of Lord Alfred Douglas?

WILDE. Yes, I did.

CLARKE. Since the time of his introduction to you in 1891 has Lord Alfred been from time to time to dine with you at Tite Street?

WILDE. Oh, yes, continually.

CLARKE. With your wife?

WILDE. Oh, yes, certainly.

CLARKE. Also at the Albemarle Club?

WILDE. Yes.

CLARKE. I think Mrs Wilde is a member of that club?

WILDE. Yes.

CLARKE. And he has also stayed with you and your family at Cromer, Goring, Worthing and Torquay?

WILDE. Yes.

CLARKE. In the year 1893 did you hear that some letters that you had written to Lord Alfred Douglas had come into the possession of a man named Wood?

WILDE. Yes.

CLARKE. Did you know this person?

WILDE. I had met him once or twice before at the Café Royal.

CLARKE. And did Wood eventually come to see you?

WILDE. No, he didn't come to see me, I met him by appointment.

CLARKE. Where?

WILDE. At the rooms of a Mr Alfred Taylor.

Lighting changes into the louche and candlelit rooms of Alfred Taylor. **WOOD** *is seen handing the letters to* **WILDE**.

I hear you have some letters of mine to Lord Alfred Douglas. You certainly should have given them back to him.

WOOD. I suppose you think very badly of me? Here are the letters.

He hands over the letters and eyes **WILDE** *closely.*

WILDE. Thank you. *(glances at the letters)* I do not consider these letters of any importance.

WOOD. They were stolen from me the day before yesterday by a man called Allen. I had to employ a private detective to get them back. They were going to try and get some money from you for them.

WILDE. Well, I do not consider that they are of any value at all.

WOOD. Please, Mr Wilde. I'm already out of pocket. *(WILDE says nothing)* Look, I'm frightened to stay in London as this Allen fellow is threatening me. I'd like to go to

New York and find some work there. Twenty pounds should do it.

WILDE. What better opportunities can you find in New York than in London?

WOOD. I've got to leave London or they'll have me! I can't find nothing straight to do here. You've been to America and you done alright. You won't hear from me again, I swear.

WILDE. Well, here's fifteen pounds. That should more than cover your passage to New York.

WILDE walks back into the box.

That ended the interview and eventually another man came with the fourth letter. I was told by my servant that a Mr Allen wished to see me on particular business…

Enter **WILLIAM ALLEN**. *He holds up a copy of the 'prose-poem' letter so* **WILDE** *can see it.*

I see you have come about my beautiful letter to Lord Alfred Douglas. I'm glad to hear it as I consider it to be a work of art.

ALLEN. A very curious construction could be put upon this letter, Mr Wilde.

WILDE. Art is rarely intelligible to the criminal classes.

ALLEN. A certain gentleman has offered me sixty pounds for it.

WILDE. Well, if you take my advice you will go to that man and sell my letter to him for sixty pounds.

ALLEN. Eh?

WILDE. I myself have never received so large a sum for any prose-work of that very small length, but I am glad to find that there is someone in England who considers that a letter of mine is worth sixty pounds.

ALLEN. *(somewhat taken aback)* The man is out of town at present.

WILDE. He is sure to come back. Take my advice; go to this man who offers sixty pounds. Don't bother me about it.

ALLEN. Look, Mr Wilde, I'm very hard up. I haven't a single penny and I've been trying to find you for some time to talk about this matter...

WILDE. I cannot really be bothered any more about this letter. I don't care twopence for it.

Turns as if to walk away.

ALLEN. Here you are!

He proffers the letter. **WILDE** *hesitates then takes it.*

WILDE. Why are you giving it back to me?

ALLEN. There's no use trying to rent you as you only laugh at us.

WILDE. *(looking at the letter)* Well, I think it quite unpardonable that better care was not taken of an original manuscript of mine. This letter is a prose-poem and will shortly be published in sonnet form in a delightful magazine. I will send you a copy. *(he goes to leave but* **ALLEN** *coughs plaintively)* Here's half a sovereign for your trouble. I am afraid you are leading a wonderfully wicked life.

ALLEN. There is good and bad in everyone of us, Mr Wilde.

WILDE. Ah, You're a born philosopher. *(exit* **ALLEN***)* A curious construction? *(he reads)* 'I know Hyacinthus whom Apollo loved so madly was you in...' well, perhaps.

He folds up the letter, places it in his jacket pocket and returns to the box.

CLARKE. The letter then was in your possession and you have produced it here in court today?

WILDE. Yes.

CLARKE. Now I pass to the year 1894. I think at the end of June, there was an interview between you and Lord Queensberry.

WILDE. Yes.

CLARKE. Where was that?

WILDE. At 16 Tite Street.

CLARKE. About what time in the day was it?

WILDE. About 4 o'clock in the afternoon.

CLARKE. What room did this interview take place in?

WILDE. My library on the ground floor. Lord Queensberry was standing by the window. I walked over to the fireplace...

    QUEENSBERRY *enters.*

QUEENSBERRY. Sit down!

WILDE. I don't allow you to talk like that to me in my house or anywhere else.

QUEENSBERRY. I hear you were thoroughly well blackmailed last year for a disgusting sodomitic letter that you wrote to my son.

WILDE. The letter was a beautiful letter and I never write except for publication.

QUEENSBERRY. You were both kicked out of The Savoy Hotel at a moments notice for your disgusting conduct.

WILDE. That is a lie.

QUEENSBERRY. You have taken furnished rooms for him in Piccadilly.

WILDE. I haven't done anything of the kind! Lord Queensberry, do you seriously accuse your son and me of sodomy?

QUEENSBERRY. I don't say that you are it, but you look it and you pose as it, which is just as bad. If I catch you and my son together again in any public restaurant, I will thrash you.

WILDE. *(he rings for his servant, Arthur)* I don't know what the Queensberry rules are, but the Oscar Wilde rule is to shoot at sight. Lord Queensberry leave my house.

QUEENSBERRY. I will not!

ARTHUR enters. **WILDE** *points out* **QUEENSBERRY**.

WILDE. Arthur, this is the Marquess of Queensberry the most infamous brute in London. You are never to allow him to enter my house again. Should he attempt to come in, you must send for the police.

QUEENSBERRY. You miserable creature. You're a damned cur and coward of the Lord Rosebery type.

He leaves and **WILDE** *returns to the box.*

CLARKE. Was it the fact that you had taken rooms in Piccadilly for his son?

WILDE. No, quite untrue.

CLARKE. Now, there are only two other topics I have to mention. It is suggested here that you are responsible for the publication of a magazine called *The Chameleon* in which certain 'Phrases and Philosophies for the Use of the Young' and certain aphorisms of yours appear on the first three pages.

WILDE. Yes.

CLARKE. Had you anything to do with the ownership or the preparation of or publication of that number of *The Chameleon* except in sending your contribution.

WILDE. Nothing whatsoever, I had nothing to do with it – nothing.

CLARKE. The other matter, which is mentioned is this book called *The Picture of Dorian Gray* with your name upon the title page.

Holds up a copy of The Picture of Dorian Gray *in book form.*

WILDE. Yes.

CLARKE. Was it originally published in serial form?

WILDE. It was first published in *Lippincott's*, an American magazine, of the previous year.

CLARKE. Then, was it with alterations or additions or what – was any change made – when it was published in this country?

WILDE. In book form there were several changes made; new chapters were, in fact, added.

CLARKE. This is the only volume, I think, with your name upon the title page that has been published?

WILDE. Yes

CLARKE. And was it somewhat widely noticed and reviewed?

WILDE. Yes, very much – very much so indeed.

CLARKE. And has it been in circulation and on sale from that time to this?

WILDE. From that time to this.

CLARKE. Now, I need not trouble you with further questions but I think I may ask you this: Your attention has been called I think to the statements, which are made in this plea here?

WILDE. Yes.

CLARKE. Referring to different persons and impugning your conduct with them?

WILDE. Yes.

CLARKE. Is there any truth whatever in any of those accusations?

WILDE. There is no truth whatsoever in any one of them.

> **CLARKE** *takes his seat and* **EDWARD CARSON** *rises to cross-examine* **WILDE**.

CARSON. You stated at the commencement of your examination that you were thirty-nine years of age. I think you are over forty, isn't that so?

WILDE. I don't think so. I think I am either thirty-nine or forty – forty my next birthday. (**CARSON** *produces and holds up* **WILDE**'s *birth certificate*). If you have my certificate there that settles the matter.

CARSON. You were born I believe on the 16th of October 1854?

WILDE. Yes, I have no intention of posing for a younger man at all. I try to be correct in the date.

CARSON. It makes you somewhat over forty.

WILDE. Very well.

CARSON. May I ask you, do you happen to know what age Lord Alfred Douglas was or is?

WILDE. Lord Alfred Douglas was, I think, twenty-four his last birthday. (*with slight sarcasm*) I think he will be twenty-five his next birthday.

CARSON. May I take it that when you knew him first he was something about twenty or twenty-one?

WILDE. Yes.

CARSON. Now, before Lord Queensberry visited you at your house in Tite Street, had you had a letter from him saying that he did not desire you to continue your acquaintance with his son?

WILDE. No, I received no such letter.

CARSON. Are you quite sure?

WILDE. Quite sure.

CARSON. But you had no doubt whatsoever after the interview in Tite Street that, whether rightly or wrongly, he didn't wish that association to continue?

WILDE. Yes.

CARSON. I think I may take it, Mr Wilde, that notwithstanding his protests upon occasion you have continued very intimate with Lord Alfred Douglas down to the present time?

WILDE. Down to the present moment, certainly.

CARSON. Staying with him at many places.

WILDE. Yes.

CARSON. Oxford?

WILDE. Yes.

CARSON. Brighton?

WILDE. Yes.

CARSON. You were staying at Brighton, I think, when you wrote your article for *The Chameleon* magazine.

WILDE. No – you mean my contribution.

CARSON. Your 'Phrases and Philosophies for the Use of the Young'?

WILDE. No, it was not written there.

CARSON. You understood what I meant. You observed, I suppose, in *The Chameleon* that there were also contributions from Lord Alfred Douglas?

WILDE. Yes.

CARSON. Did he show them to you before he sent them to *The Chameleon*?

WILDE. No.

CARSON. You had never seen them?

WILDE. I had seen them – yes.

CARSON. Did you approve of them?

WILDE. I think they are exceedingly beautiful poems both of them.

CARSON. Exceedingly beautiful poems?

WILDE. Yes.

CARSON. They are the one 'In Praise of Shame' and the other 'Two Loves'?

WILDE. Yes.

CARSON. Two loves were two boys?

WILDE. Yes.

CARSON. One calls his love 'true love'? The other boy's love is 'shame'?

WILDE. Yes.

CARSON. Did that suggest to you –

WILDE. Are you quoting from the poem?

CARSON. Yes, I have it here:

"'I am true Love, I fill the hearts of boy and girl with mutual flame." Then sighing said the other, "Have thy will, I am the Love that dare not speak its name."'

WILDE. Yes, that is the last line.

CARSON. Do you think that made improper suggestions?

WILDE. No.

CARSON. Nothing whatsoever?

WILDE. Certainly not.

> CARSON *looks incredulously at the jury and takes up*
> The Chameleon.

CARSON. Now, these 'Phrases and Philosophies' of yours in the first article in *The Chameleon* – your 'contribution' –

WILDE. Yes.

CARSON. Do you think that they were maxims likely to tend to immorality amongst young men?

WILDE. My work never aims at producing any effect but that of literature.

CARSON. Literature?

WILDE. Yes, literature.

CARSON. May I take it that you are not concerned whether it has a moral or an immoral effect?

WILDE. I don't myself believe that any book or work of art ever produces any effect on conduct at all.

CARSON. You do not consider when you come to write these things, the effect in creating morality or immorality?

WILDE. Certainly not.

CARSON. You pose as not being concerned about morality?

WILDE. I don't know whether you use the word 'pose' in any particular sense.

CARSON. 'Pose' is a favourite word of yours I think.

WILDE. Is it? I have no 'pose' in the matter. I am concerned entirely with literature, that is with Art. The aim is not to do good or to do evil, but to try and make a thing that will have some quality of beauty, and of wit and of emotion.

CARSON. Listen, sir. Here is one of your 'Phrases and Philosophies for the Use of the Young': 'Wickedness is a myth invented by good people to account for the curious attractiveness of others.' Do you think that's true?

WILDE. I rarely think that anything I write is true.

CARSON. Did you say 'rarely'?

WILDE. I said 'rarely'. I might have said never.

CARSON. Nothing you ever write is true?

WILDE. Not true in the sense of correspondence to fact; to represent wilful moods of paradox, of fun, nonsense, of anything at all – but not true in the actual sense of correspondence to actual facts of life, certainly not; I should be very sorry to think it.

CARSON. 'If one tells the truth one is sure sooner or later to be found out'?

WILDE. Yes, I think that is a very pleasing paradox, but I don't set any high store on that as an axiom.

CARSON. Do you think it was a good educational axiom for youth?

WILDE. Anything that stimulates thought in people of any age is good for them.

CARSON. Whether moral or immoral?

WILDE. Thought is never either one or the other.

CARSON. No such thing as an immoral thought?

WILDE. No, there are immoral emotions, but thought is an intellectual thing, at least that is the way I use the word.

CARSON. Listen to this: 'Pleasure is the only thing one should live for, nothing ages like happiness.' Do you think pleasure is the only thing that one should live for?

WILDE. I think self-realisation is the primal aim of life. I think that to realise one's self through pleasure is finer than to realise oneself through pain. I was, on that subject, entirely on the side of the ancients – the Greeks.

CARSON. 'There is something tragic about the enormous number of young men there are in England at the present moment who start life with perfect profiles, and end by adopting some useful profession.' Is that a 'Phrase and Philosophy for the Young'?

WILDE. I should think the young had enough sense of humour to see the beautiful nonsense.

CARSON. Now, as regards *Dorian Gray*, I think you told us that you first published that in *Lippincott's Magazine?*

WILDE. Yes.

CARSON. There were a good many criticisms of it?

WILDE. Yes, there were.

CARSON. And I think that you took notice of one of those yourself?

WILDE. Of several of them.

CARSON. I only know of one. The critic says: 'The story, which deals with matters only fitted for the Criminal Investigation Department or a hearing in camera, is discreditable alike to author and editor. Mr Wilde has brains and art and skill but if he can write for none but outlawed noblemen and perverted telegraph boys, the sooner he takes to tailoring or some other decent trade, the better for his own reputation and the public morals.'

WILDE. Yes. It was in the *Scots Observer*.

CARSON. You wrote an answer to that, and you say at the end:

WILDE. 'It was necessary, sir, for the dramatic development of this story to surround Dorian Gray with an atmosphere of moral corruption. Otherwise the story would have no meaning and the plot no issue. Each man sees his own sin in Dorian Gray. What Dorian Gray's sins are, no one knows. He who finds them has brought them.'

CARSON. Then, you left it open to be inferred, I take it, that the sins of Dorian Gray, some of them, may have been sodomy?

WILDE. That is according to the temper of each one who reads the book; he who has found the sin has brought it.

CARSON. Then, I take it that some people upon reading the book, at all events, might reasonably think that it did deal with sodomy?

WILDE. Some people might think so. Whether it would be reasonable or not…

CARSON. The second edition of the story that was brought out after these criticisms, I think, was modified and purged a good deal?

WILDE. No, I say there were additions made in one case or two – in one case, certainly, it had been pointed out to me not by any newspaper criticism or anything, but by the only critic of this century I set high, Mr Walter Pater. He had pointed out to me that a certain passage was liable to misconstruction.

CARSON. In what respect?

WILDE. (*hesitantly*) That it would convey the impression that the sin of Dorian Gray was sodomy.

Spotlight on **WILDE** *and we hear a voiceover of the following lines from the performance of* Earnest.

JACK. As a high moral tone can hardly be said to conduce very much to either one's health or one's happiness, in order to get up to town I have always pretended to have a younger brother of the name of Ernest who lives in the Albany, and gets into the most dreadful scrapes. That, my dear Algy, is the whole truth pure and simple.

WILDE. The truth is rarely pure and never simple. Modern life would be very tedious if it were either, and modern literature a complete impossibility!

Audience laughter, which fades back into the courtroom.

CARSON. In your introduction to *Dorian Gray* you state 'There is no such thing as a moral or immoral book. Books are all well written or badly written. That is all'. That expresses your view?

WILDE. My view of art yes.

CARSON. May I take it that no matter how immoral a book was, if it was well written it would be a good book?

WILDE. I say if a book is well written, that is if a work of art is beautiful, the impression that it produces is a sense of beauty, which is the very highest sense that I think human beings are capable of. If it is a badly made work of art, whether it be a statue or whether it be a book, it produces a sense of disgust; that is all.

CARSON. A well written book putting forth sodomitical views might be a good book?

WILDE. No work of art ever puts forward views of any kind. Views belong to people who are not artists. There are no views in a work of art.

CARSON. Let us say a sodomitical novel might be a good book according to you.

WILDE. I don't know what you mean by a sodomitical novel.

CARSON. Don't you? I will suggest to you *Dorian Gray*. Is that open to the interpretation of being a sodomitical book?

WILDE. Only to brutes – only to the illiterate.

CARSON. The affection and the love that is pictured of the artist towards Dorian Gray in this book of yours might lead an ordinary individual to believe it had a sodomitical tendency might it not?

WILDE. I have no knowledge of the ordinary individual.

CARSON. Oh, I see. But you do not prevent the ordinary individual from buying your book.

WILDE. I have never discouraged them.

CARSON. Would you just consider this passage. It is where the artist confesses his love to Dorian Gray. I believe this was left out of the purged edition afterwards.

WILDE. I deny the expression 'purged'.

CARSON. You don't call it purged but we will see.

"'Let us sit down, Dorian," said Hallward, looking pale and pained. "I will sit in the shadow and you shall sit in the sunlight. Our lives are like that. It is quite true that I have worshiped you with far more romance of feeling than a man usually gives to a friend. Somehow I had never loved a woman. I suppose I never had time. Well, from the moment I met you, your personality had the most extraordinary influence over me. I quite admit that I adored you madly, extravagantly, absurdly. "'

Do you mean to say that that passage describes a natural feeling of one man towards another?

WILDE. It describes the influence produced on an artist by a beautiful personality. Dorian Gray is a most remarkable personality.

CARSON. May I take it that you yourself as an artist have never known the feeling towards a younger man that is described there?

WILDE. I think it is perfectly natural for any artist to intensely admire and to love a younger man. I think it is an incident in the life of almost every artist.

CARSON. Is it an incident in your life?

WILDE. I will not answer about an entire passage. Pick out each sentence and ask me what I mean.

CARSON. I will. 'I quite admit that I adored you madly.' Have you ever adored a young man, some twenty-one years younger than yourself, madly?

WILDE. I have loved one friend in my life.

CARSON. You asked me to take your own phrase 'adored'.

WILDE. I prefer 'loved' – that is higher.

CARSON. Never mind going higher. Keep down to the level of your own words.

WILDE. Keep your own words to yourself. Leave me mine. Don't put words to me I haven't said.

CARSON. I beg your pardon. I am putting your own words at your own request. I want an answer to this simple question. Have you ever madly adored a beautiful male person many years younger than yourself?

WILDE. I have never given adoration to anybody except myself.

CARSON. I am sure you think that is a very smart thing?

WILDE. I don't at all. I object strongly. I object strongly to you not listening to my answers.

CARSON. I ask you 'yes' or 'no', sir, to my question?

WILDE. I have given it to you. I have never adored any young man younger than myself or any person older than myself of any kind. I do not adore them. I either love a person or do not love them.

CARSON. Then, you never had that feeling that you depict there?

WILDE. No, it was borrowed from Shakespeare I regret to say.

CARSON. *(incredulously)* From Shakespeare?

WILDE. Yes, from Shakespeare's sonnets.

CARSON. 'I adored you madly, extravagantly'?

WILDE. Yes.

CARSON. Have you ever extravagantly adored?

WILDE. Do you mean financially or emotionally?

CARSON. Financially – do you think we are talking here of finance?

WILDE. I don't know what you are talking about.

CARSON. Don't you?

WILDE. You must ask me a plain question.

CARSON. I hope I will make myself very plain before I am done. *(Slight pause)* I believe you have written an article pointing out that Shakespeare's sonnets were practically sodomitical.

WILDE. On the contrary, Mr Carson, I wrote an article to prove that they were not so. I explained that the love of Shakespeare to the young man to whom he dedicated them was the love of an artist for a personality, which I imagine to be a part of his art. There are people in the world who cannot understand the intense devotion and affection and admiration that an artist can feel for a wonderful and beautiful person, or for a wonderful and beautiful mind. Those are the conditions under which we live. I regret them.

We hear a voiceover of the following lines from the performance of Earnest.

GWENDOLEN. Mr Worthing, there is just one question I would like to put to you. Where is your brother Ernest. We are both engaged to be married to your brother Ernest, so it is a matter of some importance to us to know where your brother Ernest is at present…

WILDE. It is very painful for me to be forced to speak the truth. It is the first time in my life that I have ever been reduced to such a painful position, and I am really quite inexperienced in doing anything of the kind.

Audience laughter, which fades back into the courtroom.

CARSON. I want to ask you a few questions about the letter, which my learned friend introduced in your examination this morning. I understand that this letter, which you wrote to Lord Alfred Douglas, found its way into the hands of certain individuals who attempted to blackmail you.

WILDE. Yes.

CARSON. And that you were determined to face them on the subject because you had already decided to turn the letter into a sonnet for publication.

WILDE. Yes.

CARSON. Was that an ordinary letter?

WILDE. Ordinary? I should think not.

CARSON. 'My own boy'. Was that ordinary?

WILDE. No, I say it is not ordinary.

CARSON. Just wait. I want to see what is extraordinary about it. You would think, I suppose, Mr Wilde, that a man of your age to address a man nearly twenty years younger as 'My own boy' would be an improper thing?

WILDE. No, not if I was fond of him. I don't think so.

CARSON. Not in the least?

WILDE. If I call people my boy – I say 'My own boy'. I was fond of Lord Alfred Douglas. I had always been.

CARSON. Did you adore him?

WILDE. No, I loved him.

CARSON. 'Your sonnet is quite lovely. It is a marvel that those red rose-leaf lips of yours should be made no less for music of song than for madness of kissing.'

WILDE. Yes.

CARSON. Do you mean to tell me, sir, that that was a natural and proper way to address a young man?

WILDE. I think it was a beautiful letter. If you ask me whether it is proper, you might as well ask me whether King Lear is proper, or a sonnet of Shakespeare is proper.

CARSON. But apart from art?

WILDE. Ah! I cannot do that.

CARSON. But apart from art?

WILDE. I cannot answer any question apart from art.

CARSON. Suppose a man now who was not an artist had written this letter to a handsome young man, as I believe Lord Alfred Douglas is, some twenty years younger than himself – would you say that it was a proper and natural kind of letter to write to him?

WILDE. A man who was not an artist could never have written that letter.

CARSON. Why?

WILDE. Because nobody but an artist could write it.

CARSON. Supposing a man had an unholy and immoral love towards a boy or a young fellow; I believe that has happened?

WILDE. Yes.

CARSON. And he addressed him in the language that would perhaps probably be used in a love letter – he might use those words?

WILDE. He certainly could not use such language as I used unless he was a man of letters and an artist. He could not do it.

CARSON. There is nothing very –

WILDE. I disagree with you there is everything –

CARSON. I was just going to suggest there is nothing very wonderful in this: 'that those red rose-leaf lips of yours should be made no less for music of song than for madness of kissing'.

WILDE. Literature depends upon how it is read, Mr Carson. It must be read in a different way.

CARSON. Is there anything wonderful in that.

WILDE. Yes, I think it is a beautiful phrase.

CARSON. A beautiful phrase?

WILDE. Yes, a beautiful phrase.

CARSON. 'Your slim gilt soul walks between passion and poetry'. That is a beautiful phrase too?

WILDE. Not when you read it, Mr Carson. When I wrote it, it was beautiful. You read it very badly.

CARSON. I don't profess to be an artist, Mr Wilde.

WILDE. Then, don't read it to me.

CARSON. And if you will allow me to say so, sometimes, when I hear you give evidence I am glad I am not.

CLARKE. I do not think my learned friend is entitled to say that.

CARSON. When he assails me as to the way I have read the letter – I have read it in a perfectly proper way.

WILDE. Any letter may sound vulgar or ignoble –

CLARKE. Kindly do not find fault with my learned friend's reading again. It disturbs the proceedings.

There is a slight pause.

CARSON. You have written, I take it, many of these letters to Lord Alfred Douglas?

WILDE. I don't know what you call 'these letters'?

CARSON. Of this particular class.

WILDE. There is no class in that letter. That is a beautiful letter. It is a poem and I have written other beautiful letters to Lord Alfred Douglas.

CARSON. Other beautiful letters? Have you written others in the same style?

WILDE. I don't repeat myself in style.

CARSON. Now, here is another letter, which I believe you also wrote to Lord Alfred Douglas. Is that a poem – is that your writing?

WILDE. Yes, that is a letter of mine. It is from The Savoy Hotel. *(lighting change as* **WILDE** *speaks the words of the letter)* 'Dearest of all Boys, Your letter was delightful – red and yellow wine to me: but I am sad and out of sorts. Bosie, you must not make scenes with me: they kill me. They wreck the loveliness of life. I cannot see you, so Greek and gracious, distorted by passion – I cannot listen to your curved lips saying hideous things to me. Don't do it. You break my heart. I had sooner be rented all day than have you bitter, unjust, horrid. I must see you soon. You are the divine thing I want – the thing of grace and genius, but I don't know how to do it. Shall I go to Salisbury? There are many difficulties. My bill here is forty-nine pounds for a week. I have also got a new sitting room over the Thames. But you – why are you not here, my dear, my wonderful boy? I fear I must leave. No money, no credit, and a heart of lead. Ever your own Oscar.'

CARSON. Is that an extraordinary letter?

WILDE. I think everything I write extraordinary. Yes, I don't pose as being ordinary – good heavens! Ask me any questions you like about it.

CARSON. I am afraid I have a good deal to ask you. Isn't that a love letter?

WILDE. It is a letter expressive of love.

CARSON. Is it the kind of letter that one man writes towards another man?

WILDE. It is the kind of letter that I have written to Lord Alfred Douglas. What other men write to other men I know nothing about, nor do I care.

CARSON. Have you got the letter from Lord Alfred Douglas to which that was an answer?

WILDE. I don't recollect what letter it was at all.

CARSON. You don't remember the letter, but you describe it as 'delightful red and yellow wine' to you?

WILDE. Oh, yes, a beautiful letter certainly.

CARSON. Have you got it?

WILDE. No, I don't think I have got it.

CARSON. What would you pay for that beautiful letter? How much would you give now, if you could get a copy?

WILDE. I don't know. Why do you taunt me with such questions?

CARSON. You really don't know? Was this letter a beautiful letter, this one of yours?

WILDE. Yes. I think it contains reproaches. It isn't like the other – a prose-poem. It is a letter expressive of my great devotion to Lord Alfred Douglas. I can say no more.

CARSON. You have told me that you wrote a great many beautiful letters: did you ever have any of them, excepting the one which was the subject of attempted blackmail, turned into a sonnet?

WILDE. I would require to read a great deal of modern poetry before I could answer that.

CARSON. Did you ever have any letter, except the one that was found out, turned into a sonnet?

WILDE. I don't know what you mean by 'the one that was found out'.

CARSON. The one, sir, for which you gave the money.

WILDE. I gave no money for that letter.

CARSON. The one which you got back?

WILDE. The one which was handed back to me.

CARSON. I ask you, sir, excepting that, have you ever had a letter turned into a sonnet?

WILDE. At the present moment, no – I cannot recollect any. (*there is a slight pause*)

CARSON. Did you become intimate with a young lad named Conway?

WILDE. *(taken aback)* I beg your pardon.

CARSON. Did you become intimate with a young man named Conway?

WILDE. Oh, yes, at Worthing.

CARSON. What was his Christian name?

WILDE. Alfonso.

CARSON. Do you know that his previous occupation had been selling newspapers on the pier at Worthing?

WILDE. No, I had no idea that he had any connection with literature in any form.

CARSON. What was he doing?

WILDE. Oh, enjoying himself in being idle.

CARSON. He was a loafer at Worthing?

WILDE. I call him a very happy, idle nature. You can call him what you like.

CARSON. Was he an artist?

WILDE. Oh, not at all.

CARSON. What age was he?

WILDE. I suppose about eighteen – about eighteen, I should think.

CARSON. How did you come to know him?

WILDE. To know Alfonso Conway? When I was at Worthing last August, Lord Alfred Douglas and I were in the habit of going out in a sailing boat and one afternoon while this boat, which was high-beached, was being dragged down by the boatmen, Conway, and a younger boy who was in flannels, were helping to draw down the boat. I said to Lord Alfred Douglas when we reached the sea: 'Shall we ask them whether they would like a sail?' and he said: 'Yes,' and they seemed very delighted and they came out for a sail. They came out every day.

CARSON. They came out every day?

WILDE. Yes, every day.

CARSON. Did you become intimate with Alfonso?

WILDE. Oh, yes. We were great friends.

CARSON. Great friends?

WILDE. Great friends.

CARSON. Did you ask this boy that you met upon the beach to lunch with you?

WILDE. Yes, he lunched with me and Lord Alfred and the other friend.

CARSON. Was his conversation literary?

WILDE. No, it was, on the contrary, quite simple and easy to be understood.

CARSON. He was an uneducated lad wasn't he?

WILDE. Oh, he was a pleasant, nice creature. He was not cultivated. Don't sneer at that. His ambition was to be a sailor.

CARSON. What was his class in life?

WILDE. If you ask me what his class in life was, his father had been an electrical engineer who had died young. His mother had very little money and kept a lodging house – at any rate she had one lodger. That he himself was the only child, that he had been sent to school where naturally he had not learned much. That was the story he told me.

CARSON. And you conceived a great fondness for Alfonso?

WILDE. A most pleasant creature.

CARSON. Did you take him one evening after nine o'clock to walk towards Lancing?

WILDE. No.

CARSON. Are you quite sure of that?

WILDE. Yes, quite certain. Yes.

CARSON. Is Lancing near there?

WILDE. It is about two miles off.

CARSON. Is it a lonely road?

WILDE. I have never been there in the daytime. It is a road by the sea.

CARSON. Did you kiss him on the road?

WILDE. Certainly not.

CARSON. Did you put your hands inside his trousers?

WILDE. No, certainly not.

CARSON. Did you give him a cigarette case?

WILDE. I think I might have – yes, that I might have done. I forgot about that.

CARSON. What did you call him?

WILDE. Alfonso.

CARSON. Did he call you Oscar?

WILDE. No.

CARSON. Are you quite sure of that?

WILDE. Yes.

CARSON. You were fond of this boy?

WILDE. I liked him. He had been my companion for six weeks.

CARSON. He had been your companion for six weeks?

WILDE. A month, I suppose.

CARSON. Did you bring this boy away with you to Brighton?

WILDE. Yes.

CARSON. How was he dressed?

WILDE. A suit of clothes I had given him – a suit of blue serge clothes.

CARSON. That you had given him?

WILDE. Yes, I did, certainly. I gave him a suit of clothes, straw hat, flannels, a book to read – I gave him a lot of things.

CARSON. You dressed him up to bring him to Brighton?

WILDE. Not to bring him to Brighton.

CARSON. You dressed him up for Worthing?

WILDE. Yes, for a regatta which he was very anxious to go to.

CARSON. In order that he might look more like an equal?

WILDE. Oh, no, he never would have looked that. No, in order that he shouldn't be ashamed, as he told me he was, of his shabby and ordinary clothes – because he desired to have flannels and blue serge and a straw hat.

CARSON. Did he look better when he was dressed up?

WILDE. Yes, he looked much nicer, much nicer.

CARSON. What did you take him to Brighton for?

WILDE. I took him to Brighton because I had promised that before I left Worthing I would take him on some trip, to any place where he wished to go, because he had been a very pleasant, happy, good-humoured companion to myself and my children.

CARSON. How was it that he was such a pleasant companion for you?

WILDE. Because he was a pleasant, bright, simple, nice nature. That is what I call him.

We hear a voiceover of the following lines from the performance of Earnest.

ALGERNON. Why is it that at a bachelor's establishment the servants invariably drink the champagne? I ask merely for information.

LANE. I attribute it to the superior quality of the wine, sir. I have often observed that in married households the champagne is rarely of a first-rate brand.

ALGERNON. That will be all Lane.

LANE. Thank you Sir.

ALGERNON. Lane's views on marriage seem rather lax…

WILDE. Really, if the lower orders don't set us a good example, what on earth is the use of them? They seem, as a class, to have absolutely no sense of moral responsibility.

Audience laughter, which fades back into the courtroom.

CARSON. Do you know Charles Parker?

WILDE. Yes.

CARSON. Was he a gentleman's servant out of employment?

WILDE. I had no knowledge of that at all. I never heard it, nor should I have minded. I don't care twopence about people's social positions.

CARSON. Even if he was a gentleman's servant out of employment you would become friendly with him?

WILDE. I would become friendly with any human being that I liked.

CARSON. How old was Parker?

WILDE. I don't keep a census.

CARSON. I am not asking you about a census.

WILDE. I don't know what his age was.

CARSON. What about was his age?

WILDE. I should say about twenty; he was young. That was one of his attractions, the attraction of youth.

CARSON. He was seventeen.

WILDE *(somewhat petulantly)* You cannot ask me a question about which I know nothing. I don't know his age, he may be sixteen or he may be forty-five, don't ask me about it. I think he was about twenty. If you cross-examine me on the question whether he was seventeen, I have never asked him his age. It is rather vulgar to ask people their ages.

CARSON. Was he a literary character?

WILDE. Oh, no.

CARSON. Was he an artist?

WILDE. No.

CARSON. Was he an educated man?

WILDE. Culture was not his strong point.

CARSON. Did you ever ask this man, with whom you were so friendly, what his previous occupation was?

WILDE. I never enquire about people's pasts.

CARSON. Nor their futures?

WILDE. Ah, that is so problematic.

CARSON. Where did you first meet Parker?

WILDE. I first met Parker at Kettner's Restaurant.

CARSON. With whom?

WILDE. With one of my friends, Mr Alfred Taylor.

CARSON. Was anyone with him?

WILDE. Yes, his brother.

CARSON. Did you become friendly with the brother?

WILDE. Oh, they were my guests. I am always friendly with my guests.

CARSON. Your guests?

WILDE. My guests, yes.

CARSON. Upon the first occasion that you saw them?

WILDE. Yes.

CARSON. You had never seen Charles or William Parker before in your life and they immediately became your guests at Kettner's?

WILDE. Yes, it was the birthday of one of my friends – Mr Alfred Taylor. I had asked him to dinner and I said: 'Bring any friends of yours that you like.' He brought these two young men.

CARSON. Did you know that one of them was a gentleman's valet and the other was a gentleman's groom?

WILDE. I didn't know it, nor should I have cared.

CARSON. Nor should you have cared?

WILDE. No, I shouldn't have cared if they were. That is your account of them not mine.

CARSON. Isn't that the class of person that they were?

WILDE. No, I thought – I am surprised to hear your description of them because they did not seem to me to have the manners connected with that class. They seemed to me both very pleasant and nice. They told me their father lived at Datchet and was a man of some wealth – not wealth exactly, but a man of some fortune there, and one of them, Charles Parker, said he was anxious to go upon the stage.

CARSON. Did you call him 'Charlie'?

WILDE. Oh, yes, certainly.

CARSON. The first evening?

WILDE. Yes.

CARSON. Was it a good dinner?

WILDE. I forget the menu at the present moment.

CARSON. Yes, but I suppose it was an expensive dinner – one of Kettner's best?

WILDE. Oh, yes, always.

CARSON. And the best of wine?

WILDE. The best of Kettner's wine, yes.

CARSON. All for the groom and the valet?

WILDE. No, for Mr Alfred Taylor whose birthday it was, who was a friend of mine, who had brought his friends.

CARSON. Did you give them an 'intellectual treat'?

WILDE. They seemed deeply impressed.

CARSON. Now, during the dinner, did you become more intimate with Charlie than with the other one?

WILDE. I liked him the better, yes, of the two.

CARSON. And did he call you Oscar?

WILDE. Oh, yes, I told him to. I like to be called either 'Oscar' or 'Mr Wilde'.

CARSON. You put him at his ease at once?

WILDE. At once.

CARSON. Did you give them plenty of champagne?

WILDE. They had whatever they wanted.

CARSON. You gave him as much as ever he could take – this valet out of employment?

WILDE. If you imply by that I forced wine on them, certainly not.

CARSON. You did not stint them with the amount of wine they would drink?

WILDE. *(indignantly)* What gentleman would stint his quests?

CARSON. What gentleman would stint his valet and his groom?

WILDE. His guests, sir, I strongly object to that description.

CARSON. After dinner did you say, turning to Charlie and in the presence of Taylor and in the presence of William his brother: 'This is the boy for me'?

WILDE. Most certainly not.

CARSON. 'Will you come with me?'

WILDE. No.

CARSON. Anything to that effect?

WILDE. No.

CARSON. Where did you go after the dinner?

WILDE. I went back to The Savoy Hotel.

CARSON. Did you bring him with you?

WILDE. No.

CARSON. Sure of that?

WILDE. Quite certain.

CARSON. Now, I must ask you, did you give Charlie Parker at The Savoy that evening two whiskies and sodas?

WILDE. No, he did not come back with me to The Savoy.

CARSON. Or two small bottles of iced champagne?

WILDE. I say he was not there.

CARSON. Had you whiskies and sodas that evening and iced champagne?

WILDE. That I have not really the smallest recollection of.

CARSON. Was it a favourite drink – iced champagne?

WILDE. Is it a favourite drink of mine?

CARSON. Yes.

WILDE. Yes, strongly against my doctor's orders.

CARSON. Never mind the doctor's orders.

WILDE. I don't. It has all the more flavour if you discard the doctor's orders.

CARSON. I ask you, on that occasion, did Charlie Parker sleep with you for several hours?

WILDE. Certainly not.

CARSON. Or get into bed with you?

WILDE. Certainly not.

CARSON. Did you give him a cigarette case?

WILDE. Yes, I gave him a cigarette case.

CARSON. Did you give him money?

WILDE. Yes, I gave him three pounds – four pounds.

CARSON. Three pounds or four pounds?

WILDE. Yes, he was hard up and asked me would I do it – I did it.

CARSON. Do you know how he was living?

WILDE. He told me from an allowance by his father of the smallness of which he complained. That is a habit of sons.

CARSON. Really? What I would like to ask you is this: what was there in common between you and this young man of this class?

WILDE. Well, I will tell you Mr Carson, I delight in the society of people much younger than myself. I like those who may be called idle and careless. I recognise no social distinctions at all of any kind and to me youth – the mere fact of youth – is so wonderful that I would sooner talk to a young man half an hour than even be, well, cross-examined in court.

A pause.

CARSON. Did you know Walter Grainger?

WILDE. Yes.

CARSON. What was he?

WILDE. A servant at Lord Alfred Douglas's rooms in Oxford.

CARSON. How old was he?

WILDE. I should think about sixteen.

CARSON. You used to go down to those rooms, Mr Wilde, sometimes?

WILDE. They were the rooms of Lord Alfred Douglas and Lord Encombe. I constantly stayed from Saturday to

Monday, I think, certainly three times from Saturday to Monday.

CARSON. Were you on familiar terms with Grainger?

WILDE. What do you mean by 'familiar terms'?

CARSON. I mean to say did you have him to dine with you or anything of that kind?

WILDE. No! It is really trying to ask me such a question. No, of course not. He waited on me at the table; he did not dine with me.

CARSON. I thought he might have sat down. You drew no distinction.

WILDE. Do you think that in the case of Lord Alfred Douglas and Lord Encombe's rooms that would have happened with the servant?

CARSON. You told me yourself –

WILDE. It is a different thing – if it is people's duty to serve, it is their duty to serve; if it is their pleasure to dine, it is their pleasure to dine and their privilege. No, certainly not.

CARSON. Did you ever kiss him?

WILDE. Oh, no, never in my life, he was a peculiarly plain boy.

CARSON. He was what?

There is a slight pause.

WILDE. I said I thought him unfortunately – his appearance was so very unfortunately – very ugly – I mean – I pitied him for it.

CARSON. Very ugly?

WILDE. Yes.

CARSON. Do you say that in support of your statement that you never kissed him?

WILDE. No, I don't; it is like asking me if I kissed a doorpost; it is childish.

CARSON. Didn't you give me as the reason that you never kissed him that he was too ugly?

WILDE. No. I did not say that.

CARSON. Why did you mention his ugliness?

WILDE. No, I said the question seemed to me like – you're asking me whether I ever had him to dinner, and then whether I had kissed him – seemed to me merely an intentional insult on your part, which I have been going through the whole of this morning.

CARSON. Because he was ugly?

WILDE. No.

CARSON. Why did you mention the ugliness? I have to ask these questions.

WILDE. I say it is ridiculous to imagine that any such thing could possibly have occurred under any circumstances.

CARSON. Why did you mention his ugliness?

WILDE. For that reason. If you asked me if I had ever kissed a door post, I should say: 'No! Ridiculous! I shouldn't like to kiss a door post.' Am I to be cross-examined on why I shouldn't like to kiss a door post? The questions are grotesque.

CARSON. Why did you mention the boy's ugliness?

WILDE. I mentioned it perhaps because you stung me by an insolent question.

CARSON. Because I stung you by an insolent question?

WILDE. Pardon me, you sting me, insult me and try to unnerve me in every way. At times one says things flippantly when one should speak more seriously, I admit that, I admit it – I cannot help it. That is what you are doing to me.

CARSON. You said it flippantly? You mentioned his ugliness flippantly; that is what you wish to convey now?

WILDE. Oh, don't say what I wish to convey. I have given you my answer.

CARSON. Is that it? – That it was a flippant answer?

WILDE. Oh, it was a flippant answer, yes; I will say it was certainly a flippant answer.

CARSON. Did ever any indecencies take place between you and Grainger?

WILDE. No, sir, none, none at all.

CARSON begins his opening speech for the prosecution in spotlight. During the speech, we see WILDE *in conference with* CLARKE *in another spotlight on the other side of the stage.*

CARSON. May it please your lordship, gentlemen of the jury, appearing in this case for Lord Queensberry, I cannot but feel that a very grave responsibility rests upon me. Regarding the card, which has put him in his present position, he withdraws nothing. He was determined, at all risks and all hazards, to try and save his son.

WILDE. Thank goodness that's over with.

CLARKE. Not quite. You know the defence may examine you again?

WILDE. Defence? It feels more like the prosecution to me.

CARSON. As regards literature his standard was a very high one. His works could really only be understood by the artist. Contrast that with the position he takes up as regards these lads. It will be my painful duty to bring before you, one after the other, those poor young men to tell their tales…

WILDE. Sir Edward, some time ago I was turned out of the Albemarle Hotel in the middle of the night and… a young man was with me. It might be awkward if they found out about that…

CLARKE. Mr Wilde, when I first agreed to act for you, I asked you on your honour as an English gentleman…

WILDE. Ah, yes but I am Irish, which is quite a different thing…

CARSON. These letters can mean only one thing, unfortunately, that Wilde has conceived this vile, abominable passion towards this young man.

CLARKE. The situation is serious. I must advise you most strongly to withdraw from the prosecution.

WILDE. Do you see no possibility of a conviction, Sir Edward?

CLARKE. None at all. As things stand the jury will inevitably believe the distraught father in preference to the playwright of dubious morality.

CARSON. I want to know, when such letters have been written by Mr Wilde to Lord Queensberry's son and Lord Queensberry protests, are you going to send Lord Queensberry to gaol?

WILDE. But no one is going to believe the evidence of rentboys and blackmailers, surely?

CLARKE. We cannot take that risk or the Public Prosecutor may ask for your arrest. I can keep the case going a little longer to give you time to get to France.

WILDE. I have just been in France. One can't keep going abroad. It makes one look like a missionary or a commercial traveller.

CARSON. Really, really, gentlemen, the thing is almost past belief, and Mr Wilde knows that we have the witnesses to prove our case and he can dare no longer deny it!

WILDE. Then as an Irish gentleman, I have little choice but to stay.

CLARKE enters the court and tugs at CARSON's gown. A few moments' whispered conversation and the case is withdrawn by CLARKE.

Blackout.

Music. We see WILDE in an armchair, drinking heavily, in the Cadogan Hotel. He looks agitated and he hears what we hear, the following lines from Earnest in voiceover.

GWENDOLEN. And certainly once a man begins to neglect his domestic duties he becomes painfully effeminate, does he not?

ALGERNON. You don't seem to realise, that in married life three is company and two is none.

JACK. You have no right whatsoever to read what is written inside. It is a very ungentlemanly thing to read a private cigarette case.

CECILY. I hope you have not been leading a double life, pretending to be wicked and being really good all the time. That would be hypocrisy.

JACK. On the contrary, Aunt Augusta, I've now realised for the first time in my life the vital Importance of Being Earnest.

As the music swells, two policemen come for **WILDE** *and arrest him, leading him off the stage.*

Curtain.

ACT II

Scene 1 – Outside St James's Theatre

Music. We see a playbill for The Importance of Being Earnest *as in Act I, but the name of the author has been crossed out so that the words 'by* **OSCAR WILDE***' are no longer visible. A bill sticker comes along and pastes over the poster the word 'CLOSED'.*

Scene 2 – Marquess of Queensberry and Journalist

JOURNALIST. Lord Queensberry, do you have a few words for the *New York Herald.*

QUEENSBERRY. Well, obviously I am delighted that the plea of justification has been proved. Immediately after the verdict, I instructed my solicitors to send our witness statements to the Director of Public Prosecutions.

JOURNALIST. Is that why Mr Wilde was arrested so quickly the same day?

QUEENSBERRY. Indeed it was. I thought he might flee the country like a coward. All the better for the country, I thought, but if he'd taken my son with him I would have shot him like a dog!

JOURNALIST. I understand you've had many messages of support from distinguished people.

QUEENSBERRY. Well, you know, I have not much to do with distinguished people, but I had a very nice letter from Lord Claud Hamilton who serves as aide-de-camp to Her Majesty the Queen. And a kind telegram from Mr Charles Brookfield, the actor, who is playing Phipps in that dreadful play *An Ideal Husband.* 'Hearty congratulations' he says. Various clubs have telegraphed also. Here's one. *(he takes out a telegram)* 'Every man in the City is with you. Kill the bugger!'

Scene 3 – Holloway Prison

WILDE *is alone in his cell.*

WILDE. I said to myself that it was nobler and more beautiful to stay. I do not want to be called a coward or a deserter. A false name, a disguise, a hunted life, all that is not for me. My children are to be sent abroad and I'm not sure when I shall see them again. It's better that they are not forced to think of me as an outcast. As for Queensberry, I suppose nobody has ever had such intense pleasure of a low order and at such a low cost as he has. It is in the cheapest of markets that he has bought his triumph. But now I'm caught in a terrible net and am so pressed by my creditors that I don't know where to turn…

Scene 4 – 16 Tite Street, Chelsea

Sound of an excited mob as an **AUCTIONEER** *conducts a flash sale of* **WILDE**'s *family possessions at his home in Chelsea.*

AUCTIONEER. So that's fourteen guineas for the mahogany writing desk, which was once the property of Thomas Carlyle and, until recently, used by the prisoner Wilde. Going once at fourteen guineas going twice. Sold to the man with the mutton chop whiskers! Our next lot is a bundle of original manuscripts by the author including the notorious *Picture of Dorian Gray* as mentioned in the recent trial. What am I bid for this? Nobody? Come now; a piece of history in the making. Well, we'll leave that for the moment. Lot 237, is a very large quantity of children's toys including tin soldiers, obviously well used. Shall we start the bidding at, say three shillings? 'Ere, put that painting down! You can't just walk out with stuff. This is a sheriff's enforcement auction!

Scene 5 – The Old Bailey

Voiceover of criminal indictment which should fade in and out over the ellipses and emphasise key phrases such as 'male person' and 'gross indecency'.

VOICEOVER. Oscar Fingal O'fflaherty Wills Wilde, you are charged that on the fourteenth day of March in the year of our Lord one thousand eight hundred and ninety-three at the Parish of St John the Baptist Savoy in the County of London you did unlawfully commit acts of gross indecency with another male person, to wit, one Charles Parker against the form of the statute in such case made… and furthermore that on the eighteenth day of November in the year of our Lord one thousand eight hundred and ninety-two at the Parish of St Ann's Soho Westminster… acts of gross indecency with another male person to wit Frederick Atkins… tenth day of January one thousand eight hundred and ninety-three… acts of gross indecency with another male person to wit one Alfred Wood… first day of September one thousand eight hundred and ninety-two… acts of gross indecency with another male person to wit one Sidney Arthur Mavor… twentieth day of February one thousand eight hundred and ninety-two… acts of gross indecency with another male person to wit one Edward Shelley…against the peace of our Lady the Queen her Crown and dignity.

WILDE *is led into court looking haggard and unkempt, quite unlike the confident man of letters we saw in the* *first half. He is spotlighted for a moment as we hear his thoughts.*

WILDE. When the Gods want to punish us they grant us our wishes. I remember saying when I was at school that there was nothing I would like better than to go down in posterity as the hero of a great court case 'Regina versus Oscar Wilde'. As a partial pagan I should have had a little more respect for the power of the Fates – stuck to writing dramas rather than trying to act out my own. But the idea of an unscripted public performance at the Old Bailey was delightful: life imitating art and the outcome unknown. I went in to fight for my art but may end up fighting for my life. My audience appears to be a jury of shopkeepers. It is the best English justice based on beer, the Bible and the seven deadly virtues…

CHARLES GILL *opens for the prosecution.*

GILL. My Lord, I, Charles Gill am for the prosecution and my learned friend, Sir Edward Clarke is for the defence. This case has been instituted by the Director of Public Prosecutions and the defendant is charged with offences against section eleven of the Criminal Law Amendment Act of 1885.

May it please your Lordship, gentlemen of the jury I must beg you to dismiss from your minds anything you may have heard or read about the prisoner and to abandon all prejudice towards either side and to approach the case with absolutely open minds and impartiality.

The prisoner Wilde is charged in connection with a number of youths who will be called before the court. He is well known as an author and resided until his arrest at a house in Tite Street, Chelsea. Despite the fact that Wilde had a house in Chelsea, he has at different times occupied rooms in St James's Place, The Savoy Hotel and The Albemarle Hotel.

Wilde was also a frequent visitor to the rooms of Mr Alfred Taylor in Little College Street, Westminster. He did not hesitate soon after his first introduction to Taylor, to explain to him to what purpose he wished to put their acquaintance. Taylor was familiar with a number of young men who were in the habit of giving their bodies or selling them to other men.

About two years ago, Taylor took at a rental of three pounds a month the upper rooms of a closed baker's shop. The rooms he had furnished in a remarkable manner, draped and furnished in a curious way. He was a man without any profession. He had no servant. The windows of the rooms were heavily draped, candles burned on through the day and the languorous atmosphere was heavy with perfume. Here men got together and here Wilde was introduced to the youths who will give evidence in this case.

On nearly every occasion when Wilde called at these rooms, a young man was present with whom he committed the act of sodomy. The case of Charles Parker may be given as a sample of the others, on which I prefer to dwell with less minuteness. And I assure you that the evidence that will be called will justify you in finding the prisoner guilty on all counts.

CHARLES PARKER *is sworn and enters the witness box. He is examined by* **GILL**.

GILL. Please state your name and age.

PARKER. My name is Charles Parker and I am twenty one years of age.

GILL. When did you first meet the defendant?

PARKER. At the beginning of 1893.

GILL. And what was your occupation at that time?

PARKER. I was out of employment then, but previously I had worked as a valet to a gentleman. My brother William was the groom.

GILL. Under what circumstances did you meet?

PARKER. I remember one day being with my brother at the St. James's Restaurant, in the bar. While we were there, Mr Alfred Taylor came up and spoke to us. He was an entire stranger. He passed the compliments of the day, and asked us to have a drink. We got into conversation with him. He spoke about men.

GILL. In what way?

PARKER. He called attention to the prostitutes who frequent Piccadilly Circus and remarked, 'I can't understand sensible men wasting their money on painted trash like that. Many do though. But there are a few who know better. Now, you could get money in a certain way easily enough if you cared to.'

GILL. Did you understand to what he was alluding?

PARKER. Yes, and I made a coarse reply.

GILL. I am obliged to ask you what it was you actually said.

PARKER. I do not like to say.

GILL. You were less squeamish at the time, I dare say. I ask you for the words.

PARKER. I said that if any old gentleman with money took a fancy to me, I was agreeable. I *was* agreeable, I was terribly hard up. Mr Taylor laughed and said that men far cleverer, richer and better than I preferred things of that kind. He said he could introduce us to a man who was good for plenty of money, and that we were to meet him the next evening. He took us to a restaurant in Rupert Street. I think it was the Solferino. We were shown upstairs to a private room and there was a dinner table laid for four. After a while, Mr Wilde came in and I was formally introduced.

GILL. Had you ever seen him before?

PARKER. No, but I had heard of him.

GILL. Tell us what happened then.

PARKER. We dined about eight o'clock. We all four sat down to dinner with Mr Wilde sitting on my left.

GILL. Was it a good dinner?

PARKER. Yes, one of the best to be had. The table was lighted with red-shaded candles. We had plenty of champagne with our dinner and brandy and coffee afterwards. We all partook of it. Mr Wilde paid for everything.

GILL. Of what nature was the conversation?

PARKER. It was general at first. Nothing was then said as to the purposes for which we had come together, but subsequently Mr Wilde said to me: 'This is the boy for me! Will you go to The Savoy Hotel with me?' I consented, and Mr Wilde drove me in a cab to the hotel. Only he and I went, leaving my brother and Taylor behind. At The Savoy we went first to Wilde's sitting room on the second floor.

GILL. More drink was offered you there?

PARKER. Yes, we had whisky and soda, and Mr Wilde then asked me to go into his bedroom with him.

GILL. Let us know what occurred there?

There is a slight pause.

PARKER. He committed the act of sodomy upon me.

GILL. With your consent? **(PARKER** *does not reply. He repeats the question emphasising each word)* With your consent? *(Still no reply)* Did he give you money?

PARKER. Yes, before I left Mr Wilde gave me two pounds, telling me to call at The Savoy Hotel in a week.

GILL. And did you?

PARKER. Yes, I went there about a week afterwards at eleven o'clock at night. We had supper, with champagne and Mr Wilde committed the same acts as on the first occasion. I stayed about two hours and when I left that time, Mr Wilde gave me three pounds.

GILL. Did you see Wilde again?

PARKER. Yes, I went with my brother to stay with Taylor at Little College Street for about a fortnight. Mr Wilde used to call there, and the same thing occurred as at The Savoy. He asked me to imagine that I was a

woman and that he was my lover. I had to keep up
this illusion. I used to sit on his knees and he used
to play with me as a man might amuse himself with a
girl. He insisted on this filthy make-believe being kept
up. He also visited me at my lodgings at 50 Park Walk,
Chelsea one night between half-past eleven or twelve.
In consequence of this incident my landlady gave me
notice to leave.

GILL. Did Wilde give you anything apart from money?

PARKER. Yes, Mr Wilde gave me some presents of a silver
cigarette case and a gold ring. I don't suppose boys
are different to girls in acquiring presents from them
who are fond of them. I pawned the cigarette case
and the ring.

GILL. Where else have you been with Wilde?

PARKER. I have also dined with him at Kettner's Restaurant.
We always had a lot of wine. He would talk of poetry
and art during dinner, and of the old Roman days.
On one occasion, I went from Kettner's, to Mr Wilde's
house in Tite Street. It was very late at night. Wilde let
himself and me in with a latchkey. I stayed the night,
and slept with him, and he himself let me out in the
early morning before anyone was about.

GILL. When did you last see Wilde?

PARKER. I last saw him in Trafalgar Square about nine
months ago. He was in a hansom cab and saw me. He
alighted and asked me how I was. He said, 'Well, you
are looking as pretty as ever.' He did not ask me to go
anywhere with him then.

GILL. And how have you been employed since?

PARKER. In August 1894, I went away into the country and
enlisted. While I was with my regiment, I was seen
by Lord Queensberry's solicitor, and he took down a
statement from me.

We see **WILDE** *in spotlight on the other side of the stage
observing what has just happened.*

WILDE. I remember when I was at Oxford saying to one of my friends that I wanted to eat the fruit of all the trees in the garden of the world, and that I was going out into the world with that passion in my soul. And so, indeed, I went out, and so I've lived. My only mistake was that I confined myself so exclusively to the trees of what seemed to me the sungilt side of the garden, and shunned the other side for its shadow and its gloom.

FRED ATKINS *is sworn and enters the witness box.*

ATKINS. My name is Fred Atkins I have been a billiard marker, a bookmaker's clerk and a comedian, but I'm not doing anything at the moment. Alfred Taylor introduced me to Mr Wilde and I dined with him and Lord Alfred Douglas at the Florence. I remember that occasion because Mr Wilde kissed the waiter. He then asked me to go to Paris with him. We were seated at the table, and he put his arm round me and said he liked me. I arranged to meet him two days later at Victoria Station, and went to Paris as his private secretary. We stayed at 29 boulevard des Capucines, and had two rooms there, a bed-sitting-room and a bedroom, one leading into the other. The day after we arrived, I did some copying for Mr Wilde and afterwards I lunched at the Café Julien with him. Next day we went to a hairdresser's and I had my hair curled. I didn't know I was going to have it curled, Mr Wilde did it on his own account. He was talking to the man in French all the time.

Later, I went to the Moulin Rouge. Mr Wilde told me not to go but I went. He said I shouldn't go to see those women, as women were the ruin of young fellows. He spoke several times about the same subject, and always to the same effect. I got back to the hotel very late. I went into Mr Wilde's bedroom and he was in bed with another gentleman so I went to bed by myself. Next morning, while I was still in bed, Mr Wilde came into my room and asked me about the Moulin Rouge. I told him I'd enjoyed myself. He said: 'Shall I come into the bed with you?' I said it was time to get up.

After a couple of days, I returned to London with Mr Wilde and he gave me some money and a silver cigarette case.

SIR EDWARD CLARKE *cross-examines the witness.*

CLARKE. Have you seen Mr Wilde since you returned from Paris?

ATKINS. Yes, I have since visited him at Tite Street and once at St James's Place. Mr Wilde also called on me at Osnaburgh Street where I was living.

CLARKE. You were ill at Osnaburgh Street, I believe?

ATKINS. Yes. I had smallpox and was removed to the hospital ship. Before I went, I wrote to Mr Wilde requesting him to come and see me, and he did so. I was removed to the hospital ship the next day.

CLARKE. Where did you last see him?

ATKINS. At the St James's Theatre when he came forward at the end of *The Importance of Being Earnest*.

CLARKE. Did any impropriety ever take place between you and Mr Wilde?

ATKINS. Never.

ATKINS *moves to leave the box but is stopped by* **CLARKE***'s next question.*

CLARKE. Have you ever lived with a man named Burton?

ATKINS. Yes, at Osnaburgh Street, Tachbrook Street, and other places.

CLARKE. What was he?

ATKINS. A bookmaker. I acted as his clerk when he went to the races… I have also appeared at music halls.

CLARKE. Have you also been engaged in the business of blackmailing?

ATKINS. I don't remember.

CLARKE. Think!

ATKINS. I never got money in that way.

CLARKE. Has Burton not obtained money from persons on the ground that they have committed acts of an indecent nature with you?

ATKINS. No, sir.

CLARKE. That being your answer, I must particularise. On the 9th of June 1891, did you and Burton obtain a large sum of money from a Birmingham gentleman?

ATKINS. Certainly not!

CLARKE. What names have you gone by apart from Atkins?

ATKINS. I have a stage name. I have sometimes called myself Frederick St Denis.

CLARKE. *(writing on a piece of paper and handing it up)* Do you know that name?

ATKINS. No.

CLARKE. Do you know anything about a Birmingham gentleman?

ATKINS. No.

CLARKE. Where were you living on 9th June 1891?

ATKINS. In Lennox Gardens, Chelsea.

CLARKE. On that date did a Birmingham gentleman come with you to the rooms you were living at, and did Burton come in and threaten him, and did you and he get a large sum of money from that gentleman?

ATKINS. Certainly not. Nothing of the kind ever took place.

CLARKE. And did you take that gentleman's watch and chain and give it to Burton?

ATKINS. No.

CLARKE. Did not that Birmingham gentleman give Burton a cheque for two-hundred pounds made out in the name of St Denis, which he supposed to be your name?

ATKINS. No, I swear the thing never happened.

CLARKE. Were you and Burton ever taken to Rochester Row Police Station?

ATKINS. No.

CLARKE. My Lord, I have here a charge sheet from Rochester Row Police Station dated 10th of June 1891. Now Mr. Atkins, I warn you to attend and to be very careful. I am going to ask you a question. Think before you reply! Were you and Burton taken by two constables, 369A and 500A – you have probably forgotten their numbers – to Rochester Row Police Station and charged with demanding money from a gentleman with menaces?

ATKINS. I was not charged with that.

CLARKE. Was the statement made at the police station that you and the gentleman had been in bed together?

ATKINS. I don't think so.

CLARKE. Did not the landlady actually come into the room and see you and the gentleman naked or in the bed together?

ATKINS. I don't remember that she did.

CLARKE. Was that statement made?

ATKINS. Well, yes, it was.

CLARKE. You had endeavoured to force money out of this gentleman?

ATKINS. I asked him for some money.

CLARKE. At the police station the gentleman refused to prosecute?

ATKINS. Yes.

CLARKE. And you and Burton were liberated?

ATKINS. Yes.

CLARKE. A few minutes ago, I asked you these very questions and you swore upon your oath that you had not been in custody at all, and had never been taken to Rochester Row. How came you to tell me those lies?

ATKINS. I did not remember it.

CLARKE. Leave the box!

Spotlight on **WILDE**.

WILDE. People must think it dreadful of me to have entertained at dinner the evil things of life, and to have found pleasure in their company. But they were delightfully suggestive and stimulating. It was like feasting with panthers. The danger was half the excitement. I used to feel as the snake-charmer must have felt when he lures the cobra to stir from the painted cloth and sway to and fro in the air. They were to me the brightest of gilded snakes. Their poison is part of their perfection. They are intensely interesting...

ANTONIO MIGGE *is sworn and enters the witness box.*

MIGGE. My name is Antonio Migge. About two years ago, I regularly attended to massage Mr. Oscar Wilde at The Savoy Hotel. It was in a bedroom on the third floor occupied by him. It was March 1893, from the 16th to the 20th of the month. One morning on going into the room – I entered after knocking – I saw someone in bed. At first I thought it was a young lady, as I saw only the head, but afterwards I saw that it was a young man. It was someone about sixteen to eighteen years of age. Mr Wilde was in the same room dressing himself. He told me he felt so much better that morning and that, as he was very busy, he could not stay to have the treatment. I never attended Mr Wilde again.

GILL. You are employed as a masseur at The Savoy Hotel?

MIGGE. No, I am not a masseur. I am a Professor of Massage!

GILL. I see. Nevertheless, you are employed at the hotel.

MIGGE. No, I am not employed by The Savoy Hotel. I am a Professor, but I sometimes attend there to massage patients.

GILL. *(flustered)* We'll leave that. You had gone to the room at the usual time for the massage, had you not?

MIGGE. Yes.

GILL. Was the door of the bedroom locked?

MIGGE. I don't recall.

GILL. You don't recall? *(checking his notes)* At Bow Street Magistrates Court you said that it was unlocked.

MIGGE. Did I? Yes, it was.

GILL. And when you opened the door, Wilde was dressing?

MIGGE. Yes.

GILL. And in the bed you saw a young man?

MIGGE. At first I thought it was a young lady.

GILL. *(through gritted teeth)*. Yes, but then you thought it was a young man…

MIGGE. *(uncertainly)* Yes.

GILL. What colour hair did this young man in the bed have?

MIGGE. I don't remember.

GILL. You don't remember? But you saw only the head!

MIGGE. Yes

GILL. Was his hair fair or dark?

MIGGE. Yes

GILL. *(increasingly desperate)* Fair or dark hair?

MIGGE. No. I… err…

GILL. Try and remember!

MIGGE. I… umm… well… I am a Professor of Massage!

> *Music.* **WILDE** *is in the same position as before and has been an interested observer of* **MIGGE**'s *examination. He turns the playbill of* The Importance of Being Earnest *round. It reads:* 'COMING NEXT: 'THE TRIUMPH OF THE PHILISTINES BY ARTHUR HENRY JONES'.

WILDE. There are three rules for writing plays. The first is not to write like Henry Arthur Jones. The second and third rules are the same.

> **JANE COTTER** *is sworn and enters the witness box.*

COTTER. My name is Jane Cotter and I am employed as a chambermaid in The Savoy Hotel. I remember Mr

Wilde staying at the hotel in March 1893. At first he occupied No. 361 and Lord Douglas the room adjoining, No. 362. On the third morning of his stay, about eleven o'clock, Mr Wilde rang the bell for the housemaid. On answering the bell, I met Mr Wilde in the doorway of No. 361, and he told me he wanted a fire in his room. There I saw a boy of eighteen or nineteen years of age with dark close-cropped hair and a sallow complexion lying in the bed. I also found it necessary to call the attention of the housekeeper to the condition of Mr Wilde's bed. The sheets were stained in a peculiar way.

CLARKE. Miss Cotter, why do you wear eye-glasses?

COTTER. Because my sight is bad.

CLARKE. Do you use them when you go about your work?

COTTER. Oh dear, no!

CLARKE. Why do you wear them today?

COTTER. Because I thought I might have to recognise somebody.

CLARKE. Then you did not wear them when you say you saw the boy in Mr Wilde's room?

COTTER. No.

CLARKE. And you had to put them on if you wanted to recognise anybody today?

COTTER. Yes.

CLARKE. I have no further questions for this witness.

Sound of newspaper vendors in the streets of London.

VOICEOVER. Read all about it! The most sensational trial of the century! Oscar Wilde defends himself at the Old Bailey! Irishman hooted by the mob! Wilde says jury are brutes and illiterates!

SIR EDWARD CLARKE *opens for the defence.*

CLARKE. May it please your Lorship, gentleman of the jury, my learned friend has asked you to dismiss from your minds anything you may have seen in the newspapers.

In saying that, he was quite fair. However, this case has been commented on by a large section of the press in a way that I think is disgraceful. Such conduct is calculated to imperil the administration of justice and is in the highest degree prejudicial to the interests of Mr Wilde.

I must remind you that it was entirely my client's act in charging Lord Queensberry with criminal libel, which has brought the matter before the public and placed Mr Wilde in his present position of peril. I myself was responsible for the advice given to Mr Wilde for the course taken in withdrawing from that charge of libel. It is partly owing to that fact that I am here again on Mr Wilde's behalf to meet the accusation which could not be tried properly then. Men who have been charged with the offences alleged against Mr Wilde shrink from an investigation and in my submission, the fact of Mr Wilde taking the initiative of a public trial is evidence of his innocence. On the 30th March Mr Wilde knew the catalogue of accusations, which were contained in Lord Queensbury's plea of justification. Gentlemen of the jury, do you believe that had he been guilty he would have stayed in England and faced those accusations? Men guilty of such offences suffer from a species of insanity! Insane would hardly be the word for it, if Mr Wilde really had been guilty and yet faced that investigation.

I hope that if any doubt remains in your minds as to whether it is possible for you to acquit the defendant upon such evidence as you have heard, the doubt will at once be removed when you hear Mr Wilde deny upon oath that there is any truth whatever in the allegations made against him on the part of the prosecution.

OSCAR WILDE *is sworn and examined by* **CLARKE**.

CLARKE. Are you Oscar Fingal O'fflaherty Wills Wilde?

WILDE. I am.

CLARKE. In 1884 did you marry Miss Constance Lloyd?

WILDE. I did.

CLARKE. And from that time up to the present have you lived with her and your two sons at 16 Tite Street, Chelsea?

WILDE. Yes. I have also occupied for a time some rooms at St James's Place for the purpose of my literary work, it being quite impossible to secure quiet and mental repose at my own house when my two young sons were at home.

CLARKE. Was the evidence you gave at the Queensberry trial absolutely and in all respects true?

WILDE. Entirely true evidence.

CLARKE. Is there any truth in any of the allegations of indecent behaviour made against you in the evidence in the present case?

WILDE. There is no truth in any of the allegations, no truth whatsoever.

> **CLARKE** *takes his seat and* **CHARLES GILL** *rises to cross-examine.*

GILL. You were staying at The Savoy Hotel with Lord Alfred Douglas at the beginning of March, 1893?

WILDE. Yes.

GILL. You heard the evidence of the servants from The Savoy Hotel. Are you prepared to contradict them?

WILDE. It is entirely untrue. Can I answer for what hotel servants say years after I have left the hotel? It is childish. I have stayed at the hotel and been there constantly since.

GILL. There is no possibility of a mistake? There was no woman with you?

WILDE. Certainly not.

GILL. Had you a quarrel with Lord Alfred Douglas in that week?

WILDE. No, we never did quarrel – perhaps a little difference. Sometimes he said things that pained me and sometimes I said things that pained him.

GILL. Had he that week said unkind things?

WILDE. I always made a point of forgetting whenever he said anything unkind.

GILL. I wish to call your attention to the style of your correspondence with Lord Alfred Douglas?

WILDE. I am ready. I am never ashamed of the style of my writings.

GILL. You are fortunate, or shall I say shameless? I refer to passages in two letters in particular?

WILDE. Kindly quote them.

GILL. In letter number one you use the expression 'Your slim gilt soul,' and you refer to Lord Alfred's 'red rose-leaf lips.' The second letter contains the words, 'You are the divine thing I want,' and describes Lord Alfred's letter as being 'delightful, red and yellow wine to me.' Do you think that an ordinarily constituted being would address such expressions to a younger man?

WILDE. I am not happily, I think, an ordinarily constituted being.

GILL. It is agreeable to be able to agree with you, Mr Wilde.

WILDE. There is nothing, I assure you, in either letter of which I need be ashamed. The first letter is really a prose-poem, and the second more of a literary answer to one Lord Alfred had sent me.

GILL. Do you see no impropriety in kissing a boy?

WILDE. In kissing a young boy, a child, of course not; but I certainly do not think that one should kiss a young man of eighteen.

GILL. Charles Parker – what part of his evidence is untrue?

WILDE. Where he says he came to The Savoy and that I committed acts of indecency with him. He never came to The Savoy with me to supper. It is true that he dined with me and that he came to St. James's Place to tea. The rest is untrue.

GILL. What do you say about Alfonso Conway?

WILDE. I met him on the beach at Worthing. He was such a bright happy boy that it was a pleasure to talk to him. I bought him a walking stick and a suit of clothes and a hat with a bright ribbon, but I was not responsible for the ribbon.

GILL. You made handsome presents to all these young fellows?

WILDE. Pardon me if I differ. I gave two or three of them a cigarette case: Boys of that class smoke a good deal of cigarettes. I have a weakness for presenting my acquaintances with cigarette cases.

GILL. Rather an expensive habit if indulged in indiscriminately, isn't it?

WILDE. Less extravagant than giving jewelled garters to ladies.

GILL. And these witnesses have, you say, lied throughout?

WILDE. Their evidence as to my association with them, as to the dinners taking place and the small presents I gave them, is mostly true. But there is not a particle of truth in that part of the evidence which alleged improper behaviour. Truth may be found, I believe, at the bottom of a well. It is, apparently, difficult to find it in a court of law!

GILL. Nevertheless, we endeavour to extract it! Why did you take up with these youths?

WILDE. I am a lover of youth.

GILL. You exalt youth as a sort of god?

WILDE. I like to study the young in everything. There is something fascinating in youthfulness.

GILL. So you would prefer puppies to dogs and kittens to cats?

WILDE. I think so. I should enjoy, for instance, the society of a beardless, briefless barrister quite as much as that of the most accomplished Q.C.

GILL. I hope the former, whom I represent in large numbers, will appreciate the compliment. These youths were much inferior to you in station?

WILDE. I never inquired, nor did I care, what station they occupied. I found them, for the most part, bright and entertaining. I found their conversation a change. It acted as a kind of mental tonic.

GILL. Was the conversation of these young men literary?

WILDE. No, but the fact that I had written a play, which was a success seemed to them very wonderful, and I was gratified by their admiration.

GILL. What pleasure could you find in the society of boys much beneath you in social position?

WILDE. I make no social distinctions.

GILL. What did you do with them?

WILDE. I read to them. I read one of my plays to them.

GILL. You, a successful literary man, wished to obtain praise from these boys?

WILDE. Praise from anyone is very delightful. Praise from literary people is usually tainted with criticism!

GILL. Why did you go to Taylor's rooms?

WILDE. Because I used to meet actors and singers of many kinds there.

GILL. A rather curious establishment, wasn't it, Taylor's?

WILDE. I didn't think so.

GILL. You saw nothing peculiar or suggestive in the arrangement of Taylor's rooms?

WILDE. I cannot say that I did. They were Bohemian. That is all. I have seen stranger rooms.

GILL. Did you notice that no one could see in through the windows?

WILDE. No, that I didn't notice.

GILL. He burned incense, did he not?

WILDE. Pastilles, I think.

GILL. Incense, I suggest?

WILDE. Pastilles, I should say, in those little Japanese things that run along rods.

GILL. Rather a rough neighbourhood?

WILDE. That I don't know. It was near the Houses of Parliament.

GILL. What did you go there for?

WILDE. To amuse myself sometimes; to smoke a cigarette; for music, singing, chatting, and nonsense of that kind, to while an hour away.

GILL. You never suspected the relations that might exist between Taylor and his young friends?

WILDE. I had no need to suspect anything. Taylor's relations with his friends appeared to me to be quite normal.

GILL. I may take it, Mr Wilde, that you see no reason why the police should keep observation at Little College Street?

WILDE. No.

GILL. Now, Mr Wilde, you are acquainted with a publication entitled *The Chameleon*?

WILDE. Very well indeed.

GILL. I believe that Lord Alfred Douglas was a frequent contributor?

WILDE. Hardly that, I think. He wrote some verses occasionally for *The Chameleon*, and indeed for other papers.

GILL. The poems in question were somewhat peculiar?

WILDE. They certainly were not mere commonplaces like so much that is labelled poetry.

GILL. The tone of them met with your critical approval?

WILDE. It was not for me to approve or disapprove. I left that to the reviews.

GILL. You described them as beautiful poems?

WILDE. I said something tantamount to that. The verses were original in theme and construction, and I admired them.

GILL. Lord Alfred Douglas contributed two poems to *The Chameleon*, and they were beautiful poems?

WILDE. Yes.

GILL. Listen, Mr Wilde, I shall keep you only a very short time in the witness box. The first poem 'In Praise of Shame' ends with these words: 'Of all sweet passions shame is loveliest.' Is that one of the beautiful poems?

CLARKE. That is not one of Mr Wilde's.

GILL. I am not aware that I said it was.

CLARKE. I thought you would be glad to say it was not.

GILL. I said that was a poem by Lord Alfred Douglas and one which the witness described as a beautiful poem.

WILDE. May I...?

GILL. No! Kindly answer my questions.

WILDE. I will merely say this. It is not for me to explain the work of anybody else. It does not belong to me. But the word 'shame' used in that poem is a word used in the sense of 'modesty'. That was the explanation given to me by the person who wrote it.

GILL. Did he read that poem to you?

WILDE. Yes.

GILL. You can, perhaps, understand that such verses as these would not be acceptable to the reader with an ordinarily balanced mind?

WILDE. I am not prepared to say. It appears to me to be a question of taste, temperament and individuality. I should say that one man's poetry is another man's poison!

GILL. I daresay! The next poem is one described as 'Two Loves.' It contains these lines:

'"I am true Love, I fill the hearts of boy and girl with mutual flame." Then sighing said the other, "Have thy will, I am the Love that dare not speak its name."'

Was that poem explained to you?

WILDE. I think that is clear.

GILL. There is no question as to what it means?

WILDE. Most certainly not.

GILL. Is it not clear that the love described relates to natural love and unnatural love?

WILDE. No.

GILL. What is the 'Love that dare not speak its name'?

WILDE. 'The Love that dare not speak its name' in this century is such a great affection of an elder for a younger man as there was between David and Jonathan, such as Plato made the very basis of his philosophy, and such as you find in the sonnets of Michelangelo and Shakespeare. It is that deep, spiritual affection that is as pure as it is perfect. It dictates and pervades great works of art like those of Shakespeare and Michelangelo, and those two letters of mine, such as they are. It is in this century misunderstood, so much misunderstood that it may be described as the 'Love that dare not speak its name,' and on account of it I am placed where I am now. It is beautiful, it is fine, it is the noblest form of affection. There is nothing unnatural about it. It is intellectual, and it repeatedly exists between an elder and a younger man, when the elder man has intellect, and the younger man has all the joy, hope and glamour of life before him. That it should be so the world does not understand. The world mocks at it and sometimes puts one in the pillory for it.

GILL. My Lord the prosecution has no further questions.

Sound of newspaper vendors in the streets of London.

VOICEOVER. Read all about it! Sensational trial draws to close – Judgement day for the Prince of the Decadents – Wilde weak and dejected in the dock – Queensberry says 'It's Wilde's turn tomorrow.'

Closing statements of **CLARKE** *and* **GILL**.

CLARKE. May it please you, my lord, gentlemen of the jury I suggest to you that your duty is simple and clear, and that when you find a man who is assailed by tainted evidence entering the witness-box, and giving a clear, coherent and lucid account of the transactions, such as the accused has given today, I venture to say that that man is entitled to be believed...

GILL. It is upon the evidence only that I ask you to condemn the accused; but you will not appreciate the evidence until you know what manner of man you are dealing with. Who were his associates? He is a man of culture and literary tastes, and I submit that they ought to have been his equals and not these illiterate boys whom you have heard in the witness-box...

CLARKE. I respectfully submit that no jury can find a man guilty on the evidence of these tainted witnesses. This trial seems to be operating as an act of indemnity for all the blackmailers in London. In testifying on behalf of the Crown they have secured immunity for past rogueries and indecencies...

GILL. I must repel the suggestion that the representatives of the Crown have given either fee or reward to the youths in this case. All the prosecution has done has been to prevent tampering with those witnesses, and to ensure their attendance in Court. Naturally they have been removed secretly from place to place...

CLARKE. It is on the evidence of these harpies – Atkins and Parker – that you are asked to condemn Mr Wilde. He knew nothing of the characters of these men. It was his love of admiration that caused him to be in their society. All the dinners were perfectly open and above board...

GILL. All those visits, all those dinners, all those cigarette cases are corroboration! They confirm the truth of the statements made by these youths, who have confessed to acts for which these things were positive and actual payment...

CLARKE. You must not act upon suspicion or prejudice, but upon an examination of the facts, gentleman, and on the facts, I respectfully urge that Mr Wilde is entitled to a verdict of acquittal...

GILL. You cannot fail to put the interpretation on the conduct of the prisoner that he is a guilty man and you ought to say so by your verdict…

CLARKE. And in clearing him from this fearful imputation, you will clear society from a stain.

GILL. You owe a duty to remove from society a sore, which cannot fail in time to corrupt and taint it all.

WILDE. Listening to this court's appalling denunciation of me – like a thing out of Tacitus, like a passage in Dante, like one of Savonarola's indictments of the Popes of Rome – and being sickened with horror at what I hear, suddenly it occurs to me, how splendid it would be, if I was saying all this about myself. What is said of a man is nothing. The point is, who says it. A man's very highest moment is, I have no doubt at all, when he kneels in the dust, and beats his breast, and tells all the sins of his life.

Music.

VOICEOVER. The court will rise!

The **JUDGE** *enters.*

WILDE. All trials are trials for one's life, just as all sentences are sentences of death.

JUDGE. Gentlemen, have you agreed upon your verdict?

FOREMAN. We have.

WILDE. Society, as we have constituted it, will have no place for me, has none to offer.

JUDGE. Do you find the prisoner guilty or not guilty of an act of gross indecency with Charles Parker at The Savoy Hotel?

WILDE. But Nature, whose sweet rains fall on unjust and just alike, will have clefts in the rocks where I may hide.

JUDGE. Guilty or not guilty of a similar offence at St James's Place?

WILDE. And secret valleys in whose silence I may weep undisturbed.

JUDGE. Guilty or not guilty of an act of gross indecency at Tite Street?

WILDE. She will hang the night with stars so that I may walk abroad in the darkness without stumbling.

JUDGE. Guilty or not guilty of an act of gross indecency with a male person unknown at The Savoy Hotel?

WILDE. And send the wind over my footprints so that none may track me to my hurt.

FOREMAN. Guilty.

JUDGE. And is that the verdict of you all?

FOREMAN. It is.

WILDE. She will cleanse me in great waters, and with bitter herbs make me whole.

We hear an excited buzz go round the court at the verdict.

JUDGE. Oscar Wilde, the crime of which you have been convicted is so bad that one has to put stern restraint upon one's self to prevent one's self from describing, in language which I would rather not use, the sentiments, which must rise in the breast of every man of honour who has heard the details of these two horrible trials.

It is no use for me to address you. People who can do these things must be dead to all sense of shame, and one cannot hope to produce any effect upon them. It is the worst case I have ever tried. That you, Wilde, have been the centre of a circle of extensive corruption of the most hideous kind among young men, it is impossible to doubt.

I shall, under the circumstances, be expected to pass the severest sentence that the law allows. In my judgment it is totally inadequate for a case such as this. The sentence of the Court is that you be imprisoned and kept to hard labour for two years.

WILDE. And I? May I say nothing, my Lord?

The JUDGE signals for WILDE to be taken down. A POLICEMAN appears on stage to escort WILDE to the cells. Music. WILDE reluctantly starts to descend but the sound of applause from the first night of The Importance of Being Earnest, *as at the beginning of Act I, stops him. He turns to the audience as the applause fades up. He begins to drink in the acclaim. Then just as suddenly, it fades and he is back in the bare courtroom. The music swells as he is led away and taken down to the cells of the Old Bailey.*

Curtain.

APPENDIX

If you stage the production with more actors than three, then in Act II it is possible to have the witnesses examined and cross-examined, as happened in the first criminal trial. Below are the revised scenes with Fred Atkins, Antonio Migge and Jane Cotter questioned by both Charles Gill and Sir Edward Clarke.

FRED ATKINS *is sworn and enters the witness box.*

GILL. Will you please state your name and occupation.

ATKINS. My name is Fred Atkins. I have been a billiard marker, a bookmaker's clerk and a comedian, but I'm not doing anything at the moment.

GILL. How did you come to know the accused?

ATKINS. Alfred Taylor introduced me to Mr Wilde and I dined with him and Lord Alfred Douglas at the Florence.

GILL. Do you remember what happened that evening?

ATKINS. Yes, I remember that occasion because Mr Wilde kissed the waiter. He then asked me to go to Paris with him. We were seated at the table and he put his arm round me and said he liked me.

GILL. And did you go to Paris with him?

ATKINS. Yes, I arranged to meet him two days later at Victoria Station, and went to Paris as his private secretary. We stayed at 29 Boulevard des Capucines, and had two rooms there, a bed-sitting-room and a bedroom, one leading into the other.

GILL. What did you do during your time with Mr Wilde in Paris?

ATKINS. The day after we arrived, I did some copying for Mr Wilde and afterwards I lunched at the Café Julien with him. Next day we went to a hairdresser's and I had my hair curled. I didn't know I was going to have it curled. Mr Wilde did it on his own account. He was talking to the man in French all the time! Later, I went to the Moulin Rouge. Mr Wilde told me not to go but I went. He said I shouldn't go to see those women, as women were the ruin of young fellows. He spoke several times about the same subject, and always to the same effect.

GILL. And what did you do when you returned from the Moulin Rouge?

ATKINS. I got back to the hotel very late. I went into Mr Wilde's bedroom and he was in bed with another gentleman so I went to bed by myself. Next morning, while I was still in bed, Mr Wilde came into my room and asked me about the Moulin Rouge. I told him I'd enjoyed myself. He said: 'Shall I come into the bed with you?' I said it was time to get up.

GILL. How long did you stay in Paris?

ATKINS. After a couple of days, I returned to London with Mr Wilde and he gave me some money and a silver cigarette case.

EDWARD CLARKE *cross-examines the witness.*

CLARKE. Have you seen Mr Wilde since you returned from Paris?

ATKINS. Yes, I have since visited him at Tite Street and once at St James's Place. Mr Wilde also called on me at Osnaburgh Street where I was living.

CLARKE. You were ill at Osnaburgh Street, I believe?

ATKINS. Yes. I had smallpox and was removed to the hospital ship. Before I went, I wrote to Mr Wilde requesting him to come and see me, and he did so. I was removed to the hospital ship the next day.

CLARKE. Where did you last see him?

ATKINS. At the St James's Theatre when he came forward at the end of *The Importance of Being Earnest.*

CLARKE. Did any impropriety ever take place between you and Mr Wilde?

ATKINS. Never.

ATKINS *goes to leave the box but is stopped by* **CLARKE**'s *next question.*

CLARKE. Have you ever lived with a man named Burton?

ATKINS. Yes, at Osnaburgh Street, Tachbrook Street, and other places.

CLARKE. What was he?

ATKINS. A bookmaker. I acted as his clerk when he went to the races... I have also appeared at music halls.

CLARKE. Have you also been engaged in the business of blackmailing?

ATKINS. I don't remember.

CLARKE. Think!

ATKINS. I never got money in that way.

CLARKE. Has Burton not obtained money from persons on the ground that they have committed acts of an indecent nature with you?

ATKINS. No, sir.

CLARKE. That being your answer, I must particularise. On the 9th of June 1891, did you and Burton obtain a large sum of money from a Birmingham gentleman?

ATKINS. Certainly not!

CLARKE. What names have you gone by apart from Atkins?

ATKINS. I have a stage name. I have sometimes called myself Frederick St Denis.

CLARKE. *(writing on a piece of paper and handing it up)* Do you know that name?

ATKINS. No.

CLARKE. Do you know anything about a Birmingham gentleman?

ATKINS. No.

CLARKE. Where were you living on 9th June 1891?

ATKINS. In Lennox Gardens, Chelsea.

CLARKE. On that date did a Birmingham gentleman come with you to the rooms you were living at, and did Burton come in and threaten him, and did you and he get a large sum of money from that gentleman?

ATKINS. Certainly not. Nothing of the kind ever took place.

CLARKE. And did you take that gentleman's watch and chain and give it to Burton?

ATKINS. No.

CLARKE. Did not that Birmingham gentleman give Burton a cheque for £200 made out in the name of St Denis, which he supposed to be your name?

ATKINS. No, I swear the thing never happened.

CLARKE. Were you and Burton ever taken to Rochester Row Police Station?

ATKINS. No.

CLARKE. My Lord, I have here a charge sheet from Rochester Row Police Station dated 10th of June 1891. Now Mr. Atkins, I warn you to attend and to be very careful. I am going to ask you a question. Think before you reply! Were you and Burton taken by two constables, 369A and 500A – you have probably forgotten their numbers – to Rochester Row Police Station and charged with demanding money from a gentleman with menaces?

ATKINS. I was not charged with that.

CLARKE. Was the statement made at the police station that you and the gentleman had been in bed together?

ATKINS. I don't think so.

CLARKE. Did not the landlady actually come into the room and see you and the gentleman naked or in the bed together?

ATKINS. I don't remember that she did.

CLARKE. Was that statement made?

ATKINS. Well, yes, it was.

CLARKE. You had endeavoured to force money out of this gentleman?

ATKINS. I asked him for some money.

CLARKE. At the police station the gentleman refused to prosecute?

ATKINS. Yes.

CLARKE. And you and Burton were liberated?

ATKINS. Yes.

CLARKE. A few minutes ago, I asked you these very questions and you swore upon your oath that you had not been in custody at all, and had never been taken to Rochester Row. How came you to tell me those lies?

ATKINS. I did not remember it.

CLARKE. Leave the box!

*　　　　*　　　　*

ANTONIO MIGGE *is sworn and enters the witness box.*

GILL. Please tell the court your name and occupation.

MIGGE. My name is Antonio Migge and I am a Professor of Massage.

GILL. I believe you have practiced your 'profession' on the accused. When and where did this take place?

MIGGE. About two years ago, I regularly attended to massage Mr. Oscar Wilde at The Savoy Hotel. It was in a bedroom on the third floor occupied by him. It was March 1893, from the 16th to the 20th of the month.

GILL. Was Wilde alone in the room on those occasions?

MIGGE. Not always. One morning on going into the room – I entered after knocking – I saw someone else in the bed.

GILL. Someone?

MIGGE. Yes, at first I thought it was a young lady, as I saw only the head, but afterwards I saw that it was a young man. It was someone about sixteen to eighteen years of age. Mr Wilde was in the same room dressing himself. He told me he felt so much better that morning and that, as he was very busy, he could not stay to have the treatment. I never attended Mr Wilde again.

SIR EDWARD CLARKE *rises to cross-examine.*

CLARKE. You are employed as a masseur at The Savoy Hotel?

MIGGE. No, I am not a masseur. I am a Professor of Massage!

CLARKE. I see. Nevertheless, you are employed at the hotel.

MIGGE. No, I am not employed by The Savoy Hotel. I am a Professor, but I sometimes attend there to massage patients.

CLARKE. *(somewhat impatiently)* Well, we'll leave that. You had gone to the room at the usual time for the massage, had you not?

MIGGE. Yes .

CLARKE. Was the door of the bedroom locked?

MIGGE. I don't recall.

CLARKE. You don't recall? *(checking his notes)* At Bow Street Magistrates Court you said that it was unlocked.

MIGGE. Did I? Yes, it was.

CLARKE. So Mr Wilde was expecting you and when you opened the door, he was dressing?

MIGGE. Yes .

CLARKE. And in the bed you saw a young man?

MIGGE. At first I thought it was a young lady.

CLARKE. Yes, but then you thought it was a young man…

MIGGE. *(uncertainly)* Yes.

CLARKE. What colour hair did this young man in the bed have?

MIGGE. I don't remember.

CLARKE. You don't remember? But you saw only the head!

MIGGE. Yes.

CLARKE. Was his hair fair or dark?

MIGGE. Yes.

CLARKE. *(increasingly impatient)* Fair or dark hair?

MIGGE. No. I…err…

CLARKE. So you can't remember!

MIGGE. I…umm…well…I am a Professor of Massage!

*   *   *

JANE COTTER *is sworn and enters the witness box.*

GILL. Will you please state your name and where you are employed.

COTTER. My name is Jane Cotter and I am employed as a chambermaid in The Savoy Hotel.

GILL. Do you recognize the accused?

COTTER. Yes.

GILL. When did you last see him in your capacity as chambermaid at the hotel?

COTTER. I remember Mr Wilde staying at the hotel in March 1893. At first he occupied No. 361 and Lord Douglas the room adjoining, No. 362. On the third morning of his stay, about eleven o'clock, Mr Wilde rang the bell for the housemaid. On answering the bell, I met Mr Wilde in the doorway of No. 361, and he told me he wanted a fire in his room. There I saw a boy of eighteen or nineteen years of age with dark close-cropped hair and a sallow complexion lying in the bed.

GILL. Do you remember anything else in particular about Mr Wilde's stay at the hotel?

COTTER. Yes, I found it necessary to call the attention of the housekeeper to the condition of Mr Wilde's bed. The sheets were stained in a peculiar way.

SIR EDWARD CLARKE *rises to cross-examine.*

CLARKE. Miss Cotter, why do you wear eye-glasses?

COTTER. Because my sight is bad.

CLARKE. Do you use them when you go about your work?

COTTER. Oh dear, no!

CLARKE. Why do you wear them today?

COTTER. Because I thought I might have to recognise somebody.

CLARKE. Then you did not wear them when you say you saw the boy in Mr Wilde's room?

COTTER. No.

CLARKE. And you had to put them on if you wanted to recognise anybody today?

COTTER. Yes.

CLARKE. I have no further questions for this witness.

APPENDIX ENDS

Lightning Source UK Ltd.
Milton Keynes UK
UKOW02f2141171014

240217UK00001BA/3/P